Beijing, September 22, 2013
Wang fujing. Street.

Understanding Confucius

孔子新评

Ding Wangdao

Understanding Confucius

孔子新评

Ding Wangdao

丁往道 著

Panda Books

First Edition 1997

Copyright© 1997 CHINESE LITERATURE PRESS

ISBN 7-5071-0383-8

ISBN 0-8351-3188-2

Published by CHINESE LITERATURE PRESS

Beijing 100037, China

Distributed by China International Book Trading Corporation

35 Chegongzhuang Xilu, Beijing 100044, China

P.O. Box 399, Beijing, China

Printed in the People's Republic of China

CONTENTS
目　录

Preface

Recently, both in China and abroad, interest in Confucius has increased markedly, and there has been a growing study and discussion of his philosophy. This of course is a very positive development.

There are for saying this the following two reasons:

In the first place, studying Confucius helps one to understand Chinese history and culture. From 140 B.C., or 2,100 years ago, when Emperor Wudi of the Western Han dynasty decided to make it the country's orthodox philosophy, until the founding in 1949 of the People's Republic, Confucianism was, with one or two interruptions, the mainstay of Chinese thought. Its influence pervaded all strata of society and penetrated every field of activity, from court politics to the everyday life of the common people. It is obvious, therefore, that to understand China one has to understand Confucius.

In the second place, some of Confucius' ideas may be beneficial and useful today for China and the world. Although he was born 2,500 years ago, his views on morality, education, self-cultivation, the mean, harmony and other subjects could be considered to have a lasting value. Some contemporary philosophers regard Confucianism as one of the key factors in the rapid development of some East Asian countries and regions, and a possible solution to many of the problems besetting the world today.

Through studying Confucianism one becomes aware that the fate of a nation may be affected by a widely accepted philosophy. Confucianism was for a very long time one of the main constituents of Chinese culture. In turn, Chinese culture was one of the major forces that determined the orientation of Chinese history.

What force was it that held together as one nation such a huge population spread over such a vast area? What force was it that made them live for thousands of years, except for brief disruptions, in a single, unified country?

China's feudal economy, itself based on a natural economy, did not demand a big, unified country. Although military strength was capable of building up a large empire, it could not maintain it for long. So the reason why the Chinese people chose to live in one big country lies in the fact that they shared a unified, advanced culture. Cultural uniformity helped foster and consolidate political unification.

Chinese history has another special feature: the cultural development of the Chinese nation has never been interrupted, something that cannot be said about many other ancient civilizations. Although border ethnic groups more than once ruled all or a part of China, they nevertheless failed to alter Chinese culture in any fundamental way. On the contrary, the conquerors were themselves conquered by Chinese culture. This serves to show that military occupation and political control eventually had to give way to cultural superiority.

From this one can conclude that an advanced culture is an enduring strength of a nation, a strength that cannot be vanquished by any other force. On the other hand, cultural backwardness is often a symptom of the decline of a nation and accelerates that decline.

Today both the developed and developing countries are confronted with a multitude of problems, of which culture is a very important one. Without an advanced culture a nation is hard pressed to build up advanced economic or political systems, or indeed retain them for long, even if they already exist.

In short, in our effort to modernize China we must devote sufficient attention to cultural issues and do our utmost to develop and enhance Chinese culture. The study of Confucius should give us this inspiration.

In the preparation of this book my deepest gratitude is due to Dr. Denis Haughey of the University of Alberta, Canada, whose criticisms of the manuscript have been of the greatest assistance. I wish also to express my gratitude to Professor Pippa Tristram of the University of York, England, who read the first draft and made many corrections to it.

序

　　近来在国内外，人们对孔子的兴趣日增，研究探讨日盛。这当然是件大好事。

　　说这是好事，有以下两点考虑：

　　第一，研究孔子有助于了解中国历史与文化。从两千一百年前汉武帝宣布"罢黜百家，独尊儒术"，直到 1949 年人民共和国建立，除短时期外，孔子思想始终是中国思想的主流。它的影响遍及各阶层，深入各领域。从宫廷政治到民众生活，处处可见。很清楚，要了解中国，必先了解孔子。

　　第二，孔子思想中的某些部分，对今天的中国和世界可能有益和有用。孔子固然生于两千五百年前，但他的有关道德、教育、修养、中庸、和谐等方面的学说，可以说有永久的价值。目前已有学者认为孔子思想是促进东亚某些国家和地区迅速发达的关键因素之一，也是解决今天困扰世界的许多问题的可能的良方。

我们研究孔子，自然会注意到一种被广泛接受的思想对一个民族的命运的影响。孔子思想长期是中国文化的重要组成部分，而中国文化又是决定中国历史的走向的主要条件之一。

是什么力量使得生活在如此广阔的土地上的如此众多的人民凝聚为一个民族呢？是什么力量使得他们在几千年中，除短时期外，组成一个统一的国家呢？

以自然经济为基础的封建经济并不要求一个统一的大国。军事力量能够建立一个庞大的帝国，但并不能长久地维持它。中国人民愿意生活在一个统一的大国之中，应该说主要是因为他们享有一个统一的优越的文化。文化上的认同促成了并巩固了政治上的统一。

中国历史还有一个特点：中国文化的发展从没有中断，而世界上许多文明古国并非如此。边疆的少数民族曾经不止一次统治一部分或整个的中国，但并没有从根本上改变中国文化。相反，征服者倒是被中国文化征服了。可见军事占领和政治控制最终还是抵抗不了文化上的优势。

由此可以得出这样的结论：优越的文化是一个民

族的永恒的力量，是任何别的力量所不能战胜的。反过来说，文化上的落后常常是民族力量衰落的征兆，并使之加速衰落。

目前世界上发达国家和发展中国家都面临各种问题，其中一个主要的便是文化问题。没有先进的文化，很难建立先进的经济与政治制度；即使建立了，也难以长久保持。

归根结底，我们在使中国现代化的努力中，必须十分关注文化问题，大力推进文化建设。研究孔子应该给我们这样的启发。

在编写本书的过程中，加拿大阿尔伯达大学的丹尼斯·豪赫博士（Dr. Denis Haughey）审校了全部英文稿，提出了许多中肯的意见，帮助极大，我对他表示衷心的感谢。英国约克大学的比芭·特里斯特兰姆教授（Professor Pippa Tristram）校阅了大部分英文初稿，在多处做了改正，我向她表示感激之忱。

Chapter One: Ancient China

About half a million years ago a species of primitive man, called by archaeologists Peking Man, appeared near present-day Beijing. Traces of species of men later than him have also been discovered in many areas in the Yellow River valley. Additionally, fossils of simple farm tools made of stone, wood, and livestock bones have been discovered with these fossils of early man, suggesting that these early inhabitants were engaged progressively in agriculture and animal husbandry.

Four or five thousand years ago, or earlier, the clan system took shape. Several clans formed a tribe. Legend has it that in what is now Shaanxi Province there was a tribe whose leader was called Huangdi, the Yellow Emperor, and a neighboring tribe led by Yandi, the Fiery Emperor. Jointly they defeated a tribe to their east and killed its chief Chiyou. Huangdi is said to have invented clothes, the boat, and the cart. Yandi, also called the Sacred Farmer, is alleged to have taught people how to turn the sod with a plow, and Chiyou to have made metal weapons. At about the same time, Fuxi, another tribal leader, invented the net and designed the Eight Trigrams. Today, Chinese all over the world regard Huangdi and Yandi, who made such great contributions to the progress of civilization, as their earliest ancestors, calling themselves "Yan-Huang's descendants."

Many, many years passed before tribal alliances were made. At a meeting of tribal heads the leader of an alliance would be elected to be its military commander in war, and in peacetime, when it was time to offer sacrifices to Heaven, the Earth, the mountains and rivers, and all the gods, to preside over these ceremonies. In central China a major alliance was led by Yao, who, when old, handed over his position to Shun, and Shun to Yu, with the concurrence of the tribal heads.

Yu was popular and prestigious, for legend has it that he had tamed the flooding rivers by channelling their waters into the sea. It is said that he had travelled around the flooded areas for nine years and that he had passed his own home three times without entering it. Before he died he upheld tradition by appointing Yi his successor; however, many tribal heads preferred Qi, Yu's son. With their support, Qi put Yi to death and made himself leader, thus establishing a hereditary monarchy. This marked the transition from primitive society, where there was no family, private property, or class distinction, to a class society based on the family and private ownership.

Yu and his descendants ruled the central part of China for over 400 years. This constituted the Xia dynasty as it is called in historical works. Its last ruler was an evil man, hated by his subjects, so when Shang, a subordinate state in the east, rose in rebellion and attacked him, he was quickly defeated. Tang, the first monarch of the new Shang dynasty, ruled over the middle and lower reaches of the Yellow River. This dynasty was to last about 500 years before it was overthrown by Zhou.

It should be noted that Chinese history before the Shang dynasty, though chronicled in several ancient classics, is mainly legendary. So far no archaeological evidence has been discovered to prove that Huangdi, Yao, Shun, Yu and the Xia dynasty really existed. However, the existence of the Shang has been verified by excavated objects such as the oracle bones unearthed in Xiaotun Village, Anyang County, Henan Province, in 1899, and in the early years of the 20th century.

The Shang rulers were superstitious. Before they made an important decision such as to wage war, to worship Heaven, to go hunting, they would ask their court diviner to find out if the occasion was propitious. He would take an ox bone or a tortoise shell, drill a hole in it, and put it over a fire until cracks developed. Then he would study the cracks, which were regarded as omens foretelling the good or bad results of the action contemplated. Both the interpretation of the omens and the real result of the action, if it was performed, would be recorded in a few words carved on the bone or shell. In this way the Shang diviners unwittingly wrote faithful accounts of many significant contemporary events.

Over the years about 100,000 pieces of oracle bones have been discovered and collected in Xiaotun. The place was certainly one of the capitals, probably the last one, of the Shang, which moved its capital several times. Over 3,000 different words have been found in the inscriptions, indicating that written Chinese was already highly developed more than 3,000 years ago.

The Shang ruled over a slave society. Slaves, most

of whom had been captured in battles with other states or tribes, were forced to till the land, feed domestic animals, make handicrafts, and do household work for their masters, who, as nobles, lived an idle, parasitic life. What was more tragic was that slaves might be killed as sacrifices to the gods and their masters' ancestors, and might even be buried alive to accompany their master when he died.

During the 11th century B.C., probably in 1066, the Shang dynasty was conquered by Zhou, which had been growing from a tribe or tribal alliance into a state in the Wei River valley in present-day Shaanxi Province. For many years Zhou had been a tributary state of the Shang. Because the last ruler of the Shang, cruel and corrupt, had antagonized his ministers and subjects and the tribes under his rule, King Wen of Zhou began to make plans to overthrow him. By annexing one neighboring state after another, he expanded his territory and finally made Zhou strong enough to fight the Shang. A few years after King Wen's death, his son, King Wu, led a huge army in an attack on the Shang capital. The Shang troops, mainly slaves and poor people, revolted on the battlefield. The last king of the Shang out of desperation committed self-immolation and King Wu became the first king of the new Zhou dynasty.

When King Wu died two years later, his son was still too young to rule the country, so for seven years state affairs were directed by King Wu's younger brother, the Duke of Zhou. The political and social systems of the new dynasty were mainly designed by these three founders: King Wen, King Wu and the Duke of Zhou.

The feudal system they established was strictly hierarchical. The whole country was divided into a number of fiefdoms, most of which were assigned to members of the royal clan, but a few were given to nobles related by marriage to the Zhou rulers, and to chiefs of small states or tribes that had shown loyalty to the Zhou. Not only land, but the people on it, were given to a vassal and became his and his descendants' property. A vassal subdivided his fief into several areas and gave them to members of his clan and his confidants. These in turn gave land and people to their subordinates. It is reputed that altogether there were ten classes in the hierarchy, each class having to pay tribute and offer military and other services to the one above.

At the top of this hierarchy was the king, the master of all, people and land alike. At the bottom was the serf, bound inextricably to the land. He had to work his lord's land before attending to his own small field, and was not allowed to move out of his lord's fief. When there was a war, he had to go and fight. When his lord wanted a woman, his wife or daughter might be taken away. In short, his lot resembled that of a slave, but was a little better, for he had his small piece of land, home, family, tools, and perhaps a side-line occupation.

The Zhou ruler used two means to maintain order and stability: severe punishments to deter the serfs and common people, and rites to adjust relations among the nobles. The rites were codified rules of behavior and ceremonies. The basic principle was that the rites should never apply to the common people, and punishments should never apply to the nobility.

All these systems and institutions suited the social conditions very well and the Zhou enjoyed peace and stability for about 300 years. In King You's reign, natural calamities, internal strife in the court and attacks by border tribes brought Zhou rule to the brink of collapse in 771 B.C. In the following year, King Ping, King You's successor, moved the capital from Haojing in the west to Luoyi, now Luoyang, in the east. From then on the dynasty was called the Eastern Zhou and the period from 1066 to 771 B.C. the Western Zhou dynasty.

The history of the Eastern Zhou, 770-256 B.C., was divided into two periods. The first three hundred

years, 770-476 B.C., was called the Spring and
Autumn Period, because all the important events of
this period were recorded in a chronicle called *The
Spring and Autumn Annals*. The period from 475 to
221 B.C. was called the Warring States Period,
because there were incessant wars among the states.
The dynasty was finally brought to an end in 256
B.C., and 35 years later, in 221 B.C., China was
unified by the Qin dynasty.

All through the 500 years from King Ping's time
to the end of the Zhou dynasty, the king was the
supreme ruler in name only. Financially and
militarily weak, he was unable to control his vassals,
and from time to time he even had to ask them for
help. As a result of encroachments by various vassal
states, the area under his direct rule was becoming
smaller and smaller. Powerful states frequently
annexed smaller ones by force and fought each other
for hegemony. As wars continued, the number of
states dwindled from over 1,000 during the Western
Zhou to about 100 in the Spring and Autumn Period.

There were great social changes too. The
increasing use of iron tools helped to raise
productivity in farming. Landowners came to realize
that they could get more from their land than the
old corvee system if it was turned into plots and
rented to their serfs. Gradually their "common fields"

—fields formerly tilled by their serfs without pay — were subdivided into private fields leased out to their serfs for rent. Thus serf-owners became in effect landlords and serfs became tenants, who showed greater interest in production and enjoyed greater independence and freedom than they had as serfs.

Along with this development of agriculture, handicrafts and commerce also grew and there emerged a new merchant class. Many rich ones in big cities were influential enough to visit and bribe princes and dukes, who had to meet them and give them polite treatment.

Another group of people, scholars, also developed. Notably these came from a cross section of social classes. Before the Spring and Autumn Period, what learning there was had been monopolized by the nobility; they alone had access to the books and archives stored by the government, and other people could not share these facilities. The great political and social upheavals during the Spring and Autumn Period broke the nobility's monopoly of learning. At all levels of society — declining nobles, new landlords, free citizens, even poor people — there were people determined to study, examine various subjects, and make themselves scholars.

This was also a period when states prospered or declined, and rulers therefore urgently sought wise counsel that would help to make their states rich, strong, and stable. They turned to scholars for such help and often put them into important positions. As a result scholars were envied and other people wanted to join their ranks.

The Spring and Autumn Period was thus a time of great social change and political upheaval. It was a time of alliances and wars. States expanded or were vanquished. The rites established in the Western Zhou were no longer observed and the original social order was broken. Old beliefs collapsed and new ideas proliferated. This turbulent situation stimulated scholars of the day to devise ways to restore peace and stability. The first and most important of these scholars was Confucius.

第一章 古代中国

　　五十万年前就有人类在现今是北京的地带活动了。他们被考古学家称作"北京人"。比他们晚的人类的遗迹在黄河流域的许多地方都有所发现。石制的和木制的简单的耕作工具，以及家畜的骨骼化石，同这些原始人的骨化石同时被发现，表明他们逐步从事农业和畜牧业。

　　四、五千年前或更早一些，氏族制度便已形成。几个氏族组成一个部落。根据传说，在今天是陕西省的地区内有一个部落，它的领袖叫黄帝。附近的一个部落领袖叫炎帝。他们联合起来战胜东边的一个部落，杀死了那个部落的领袖蚩尤。据说黄帝发明衣服、船和车，炎帝（也称神农氏）教人们用犁翻地，蚩尤则制造了金属武器。大约同时还有一个部落领袖叫伏羲，发明网，并且绘制了八卦。黄帝和炎帝对文明的进步有很大的贡献，所以现今世界各地的中国人都认为他们是始祖，而自称"炎黄子孙"。

他们之后又许多年，产生了部落联盟。部落的领袖们到一起选举一个联盟领袖，在战时他是指挥，在平时则主持祭祀，祭天、地，祭山、河及诸神。中原一带有一个部落联盟的领袖叫尧。尧年老时，在取得各部落的首领的同意后，把领袖的位置让给舜，舜又传位给禹。

禹做领袖可以说是众望所归。他成功地用疏导的办法把几条大河的洪水消弥了。据说他在各地奔走治水达九年之久，曾经三过家门而不入。禹死之前，为了维护传统，指定一个叫益的人接他的班。可是许多部落的首领拥戴禹的儿子启做领袖。在他们的支持下，启把益处死，继承了父位，这样就开始了一个世袭的王朝。这个变化标志着由没有家庭、私有财产和阶级区分的原始社会向以家庭及私有财产为基础的阶级社会的过渡。

禹和他的后代统治中国中部有四百多年，史书上称之为夏朝。夏朝的最后一个君主叫桀，是个暴君，被臣民所痛恨。东方一个叫商的附庸国起来造反，对他发动进攻，很快地把他打败了。商的第一个君主汤，便统治了黄河的中、下游一带。商朝延续了约五百年，最后被周所推翻。

商以前的中国历史，虽然在一些古籍中有所记载，但主要还是传说性的。迄今还没有发现任何实物可以证明黄帝、尧、舜、禹，及夏代是确实存在过的。但是商代的历史已经被考古学家的发现所证实，这个发现是1899年及以后在河南省安阳县小屯村掘出的甲骨。

商的统治者十分迷信。他们做出每一个重要的决定——诸如作战、祭天、狩猎——之前，总要朝廷中的卜著官推断一下这个拟议中的行动是否吉利。卜著官便取一块牛骨或龟壳，在上面打一个眼，把它放在火上烤一些时候，直到裂纹出现。他研究这些裂纹，便可预知凶吉。事后他还将凶吉的预测及实际的情况用极简略的文字记载下来，刻于那块牛骨或龟壳上。这样，商代的卜著官无意中留下许多当时重要事件的忠实记录。前后共发现约十万块这样的甲骨，发现地小屯可以肯定是商代的首都之一（商代曾多次迁都），也许是最后的一个。在这些甲骨上共用了三千多个不同的字，可见汉文字在那时，也就是三千多年前，已经有了高度的发展。

商代的社会是个奴隶制社会。奴隶的来源主要是战争中的俘虏，他们被迫为主人种地，饲养牲口，制造手工物品，做家务事；而他们的主人，也就是贵族，过着懒散、寄生的生活。更悲惨的是，奴隶会被杀死来祭神或祭主人的祖先，甚至被活埋，为主人殉葬。

在公元前十一世纪（可能是1066年），商朝被周所征服。周本来是个部落或部落联盟，逐步形成一个邦国，位于现今陕西省渭水流域，在很长时期中臣属于商。因为商的最后一个君主纣腐化残忍，为臣民及下属部落所反对，周的领袖文王便有意将他推翻。文王先并吞邻近诸邦，使周强大起来。他死后不几年，继承他的武王便率大军进攻商都。由奴隶和穷人组成的商军在战场上叛乱起来，纣走投无路自焚而死。武王成了新的周代的第一个君主。

在武王胜商两年后死去时，他的儿子成王还很年幼，国事由武王的弟弟周公（名姬旦）处理有七年。周代的政治与社会制度主要是这三位开国者，即文王、武王和周公制定的。

他们建立的是有严格等级的封建制度。全国分为许多领地，大多数分封给王室成员，少数授予与王室有姻亲关系的贵族和忠于周的小邦或部落的首领。领地中的一切，包括土地和人口，统统成了受封者的财产，而且代代相传。一个受封者又将他的领地分为若干地区，分别授予他的亲属和亲信。这些人再把一块地和地上的人口分给亲属或部属。据说这样由大到小共十个等级，下一级必须向上一级进贡，并提供军事上的或其他方面的服务。

在这个等级制的顶端是周王，他是全国土地和人口的主人。在最低层的是农奴,他被束缚在土地上,不能迁出主人的领地。他必须先耕种主人的地,然后才能种他自己的一小块地。有了战事,他得去打仗。主人想要一个女人时,他的妻女可能被夺走。总之,他的命运接近一个奴隶,但稍许强点,因为他还有一块地,一个家,几件农具,还可能有一项副业。

为了维持稳定的社会秩序,周的统治者采用两种办法:对农奴和普通老百姓用刑来威慑,对贵族则用礼来调整关系。所谓礼,就是行为和仪式的规范。"礼不下庶人,刑不上大夫"是基本的原则。

这一套制度和规范很适合当时的社会条件,因而周代享有三百年左右的和平和稳定。到幽王时,自然灾害,宫廷内乱和外族入侵使周室统治濒于崩溃。这发生于公元前771年。次年周平王从镐京(今西安附近)迁都洛邑(今洛阳)。此后的周代称东周,此前(公元前1066—771)为西周。

东周(公元前770—256)的历史分两段。前三百年(公元前770—476)称春秋时代,因为这一时期的重大事件都记载在叫作《春秋》的编年史中。公元前475—221这一时期通称战国时期,因为这期间战争不断。东周最后亡于公元前256年。三十五年后,即公元前221年,秦统一中国。

从平王东迁到周亡的这五百年中,各代周王只是一个名义上的最高统治者罢了。军事上和财力上的软弱使他们无法控制分封各地的藩属,有时甚至还要请求藩属帮助。王室直接管辖的地区,由于遭到藩属国的蚕食,变得越来越小。藩属国中的强大者动辄用武力吞并弱小者,它们之间也互相进攻,以取得霸权。战事不断,属国的数目日益减少——从西周时期的一千多个减少到春秋时期的一百个左右。

与此同时,重大的社会变革也在发生。铁器的使用提高了农业的生产率。土地所有者逐步认识到把地租给农奴耕种比老式的劳役制会给他们带来更多的收入,因而由农奴无偿耕种的"公地"慢慢地变成租给农奴耕种的私地。这样,农奴主变成了地主,农奴变成了佃农。佃农比农奴有更大的生产劲头,也有更多的独立性和自由。

随着农业的发展,手工业和商业也发展起来。标志之一是一个新的阶层——商人的兴起。大城市里的富商很有影响力,他们甚至可以拜见王、公,对他们行贿;王、公们还得应付他们,以礼相待。

另一个新的阶层——士也成长起来。士就是有知识、有学问的人。在春秋时期以前,只有贵族才可能有学问,因为他们掌握了典籍。其他阶层的人没有研究学问的条件。春秋时期的社会和政治动荡打破了贵族对学问的垄断,各阶层——没落贵族、新兴地主、自由民,甚至穷人都有人发愤读书,研究各种问题,变成士。

当时各国的统治者，面对或兴或亡的形势，都迫切地希望得到富国强兵的策略。士恰好有这样的策略，所以有可能受到重用。这种情况一方面提高了士的社会地位，另一方面也激励一些人努力争取为士。

春秋时期就是这样一个社会变化、政治动荡的时期。各国之间或者和好结盟，或者兵戎相见。有些国家壮大，有些国家灭亡。西周建立的礼在很大程度上失去了约束力，原来的社会秩序已被打乱。旧的观念动摇，新的思想兴起。这种混乱局面使得有远见的士思考平定天下的途径。他们之中的第一个，也是最重要的一个，便是孔子。

Chapter Two: Life of Confucius

One of the 100 or so states of the Spring and Autumn Period was Lu, situated south of the powerful state of Qi, in present-day Shandong Province. Although small and weak Lu boasted a glorious cultural tradition. During the early years of the Western Zhou, it had been the fief of the Duke of Zhou, one of the main architects of the political system of the dynasty. As regent during King Cheng's minority, the Duke resided in Haojing, the capital, and his oldest son, Boqin, went to Lu as his heir to govern the Duke's fief. Boqin brought with him many books, documents, and ritual utensils, and promoted the rites and institutions prescribed by his father. Five hundred years later, during the Spring and Autumn Period, these were ignored elsewhere because of the princes' and dukes' scramble for power and land, and also because of the social changes; in Lu, however, most of the Western Zhou traditions were preserved.

Confucius was descended from a noble clan from Song, a neighboring state of Lu, where one of his ancestors had been involved in a power struggle in the court. When he had been killed, his son fled to Lu to escape death and made his home there. Among this man's descendants was a warrior, the lowest rank of the nobility, commonly known as Shuliang He. In fact, his surname was Kong, Shuliang being his courtesy name and He his given name.

The warrior was married twice and had several daughters and one crippled son. Custom prevented daughters from becoming heirs, and the lame son could not bring him any honor. So though already over 60, he decided to get married again, this time to a very young woman, Yan Zhengzai. After their marriage, she gave birth in 551 B.C. to a son called Kong Qiu, with Zhongni as his courtesy name. According to legend, Qiu and Ni came from Mount Niqiu, where his parents had prayed to the mountain god for a son. Confucius is his latinized name.

Confucius was only three years old when his father died. His mother then took him to Qufu, the capital of Lu, which was not far from Zouyi, the town where his father had lived. In Qufu mother and son led a hard life. However, since he showed a great interest in study, his mother did everything possible to encourage him, including buying him utensils used at sacrificial ceremonies so that he could practice the rites. But the young widow did not live to see her son established as a scholar and died when he was 16 or 17.

The lonely young Confucius, while doing what jobs he could find to support himself, devoted his days and nights to study. Later, recalling his own earlier days, he said, "At 15 I made up my mind to study," (2.4)*, and "I was a humble man when young. That is why I was able to do many menial things." (9.6) He did not specify what the "menial things" were; however, it is recounted in books about his life that he was at different times a trumpet blower for funeral ceremonies, a low official taking care of cattle and sheep, and one in charge of granaries.

As he grew up among the cultural heritage of Lu,

---

*Hereafter all quotations from *The Analects* will be indicated by the number of the chapter and that of the saying in parentheses.

and since he was an industrious learner, Confucius gradually earned a good name and a place among the nobles of Qufu. At 19 he was married and the following year a son was born. To congratulate him the duke then ruling Lu sent him a carp. Confucius considered this a great honor and named his son Li or carp.

In his day, a qualified scholar had to master the "six arts" of rites, music, archery, coach-driving, writing, and arithmetic. Rites refer to the norms of behavior and rules for ceremonies. While studying all these subjects by himself, Confucius seized every opportunity to ask questions of knowledgeable people. One entry in *The Analects* says, "When Confucius entered the temple to the founder of Lu, he asked about everything." (3.15)

Moreover, Confucius made a systematic study of the Six Classics: *The Book of Songs* (a collection of ancient folk songs and songs sung at ceremonies), *The Book of History* (a collection of ancient historical documents), *The Book of Rites* (regulations of behavior and rules of ceremonies), *The Book of Music* (ancient tunes), *The Book of Changes* (interpretations of the 64 hexagrams, which contain certain philosophical wisdom), and *The Spring and Autumn Annals*.

"At 30 I was established," (2.4) said Confucius. It

appears that he had then already studied what classics there were to study and formed his own conclusions and views on vital problems concerning history, society, and mankind. In other words, he had consolidated his own beliefs and philosophy, and hereafter the main goal in life was to practice and propagate them, and in so doing to bring light to people who were groping in darkness for the right way of life.

The method he adopted was education. He gave instruction to all who came to learn from him. By then a well-known scholar, in effect he set up a private school. This was an event of great historic significance, epoch-making in the history of education in China. Before Confucius, education, just like government positions, had been monopolized by the nobility. Their children were taught to become officials at special government schools whose doors were never open to ordinary people. Confucius was the first person in Chinese history to break this monopoly and bring education to all people, and in particular to those of ordinary birth.

From the time when he became known as a learned man, at about the age of 30, until his death at 73, he never stopped teaching. It was said that in the course of his life, he taught about 3,000 students, 72 of whom acquired a mastery of the classics and had outstanding achievements in the academic or political field.

His influence increased with the number of his students, and the rulers of Lu came to realize that it might be proper to enlist his service in governing the state. When he was 51, he was appointed a county magistrate. Soon, probably because of his excellent performance, he was promoted to the position of Chief of Public Security, a post he held for about three years.

On one occasion the Duke of Lu had a meeting with the Duke of Qi, which was a neighboring and much larger and more powerful state. As an expert of the rites Confucius was master of ceremonies and assisted his duke at the meeting. The Qi ruler had intended to force the Duke of Lu to yield to his will but was frustrated by Confucius, who, aware of Qi's plot, handled the situation with ingenuity and courage.

This victory earned Confucius so much prestige that the Lu rulers placed even greater trust in him and made him acting prime minister, responsible for the operations of the government. His way of governing quickly achieved results. Lu became a peaceful and orderly state, where "merchants never asked false prices, men and women did not mix on the road, no one took the things left on the road by other people, and travellers from abroad...felt as if they had returned home."*

But differences arose between him and the nobles who had real control of government. In reality the Duke of Lu was then merely the nominal ruler of the state with real power residing in the hands of three noble families and their confidants. Confucius, whose principle it was to obey and revere the sovereign, did not like this, and began to take steps to reduce their power. They were naturally offended. To make things worse for Confucius, the rulers of neighboring Qi sent 80 attractive female dancers and singers to the duke and the most powerful nobleman of Lu, and their interest in state affairs rapidly declined. Confronted with such an outcome, Confucius knew that it would be impossible for him to carry out his ideals about government and decided to leave. He was then 55 years old.

He started a journey that was to take him to ten states in 14 years. Accompanied by a group of faithful followers, he visited and talked with the rulers of six states about humane government, hoping that he would be employed and his principles put into practice. In these states, however, he was

---

* "Biography of Confucius" in *Records of the Grand Historian*.

either cold-shouldered, or treated politely but given no real duties. Weakened by hunger and illness, more than once he and his followers met with great difficulties and encountered dangerous situations. Upon hearing that he had been described by a stranger as a homeless dog, he smiled and said, "That is true! That is true!" Whatever happened, however, he remained unruffled and optimistic, continued to give lessons, rehearse the rites, chant poems, play the lute, and sing.

During his absence, a new generation of nobles had succeeded the now defunct older ones and assumed control of the Lu government. Urged on by those disciples of Confucius who had become important officials, the new leaders sent messengers to the state of Wei, where Confucius was staying, to invite him back to Lu. Confucius accepted the invitation and returned to Lu. He was then 68 years old.

He was certainly disappointed at having failed to translate his dreams into action in spite of the 14 years' toil. But this failure was unavoidable. At a time when invasion and annexations of territory were commonplace, the rulers of states were naturally anxious to seek counsel that would help to make their states rich and strong. Confucius' views on humane government must have sounded to them too impractical to be worthy of serious consideration.

After he returned to Lu, he no longer sought a government post, but devoted his time to teaching and editing the classics.

He must have used the Six Classics as teaching material. In his last years he edited and revised them, keeping what he thought to be true and good, and eliminating what was false and harmful, intending to make them perfect.

Note that Confucius did not write any books. At the time when he lived, it was not yet customary for an individual to write for publication. The classics he edited were made up of court documents and historical records handed down from the Western Zhou or earlier periods, and folk songs specially collected over the ages. All those works, with few exceptions, were anonymous. Moreover, Confucius himself preferred interpreting ancient principles to creating new theories. He said, "I would rather transmit than create, for I believe in and have a liking for antiquity." (7.1)

Fortunately there is a book, *The Analects*, which expresses Confucius' views and theories more clearly and more directly than these classics. Collected in it are about 500 sayings of Confucius and his major disciples, and their comments and answers to questions. Obviously they were recorded and compiled by those students who had heard Confucius talking and his disciples discussing the master's instructions. The 500 sayings deal with a wide range of vital issues: humanity and rites, government and law, education and knowledge, music and poetry, the gentleman's qualities and the small man's weaknesses. In addition, there are a few brief descriptions of Confucius' manner, lifestyle and personality.

Except for *The Book of Music*, the classics edited by Confucius survived the burning of books by the first emperor of the Qin in 213 B.C. So did *The Analects*. Since the Han dynasty they had been the most important texts for scholars of all ages, and they exerted a most pervasive influence on Chinese thought. These books, especially *The Analects*, contain immeasurable wisdom, which, like a torch, was to light the path of the Chinese for over 2,000 years. It was only at the beginning of the present century that their acceptability began to be questioned.

In his last years Confucius suffered a series of heavy blows as a result of those dear to him dying one after another. His wife had died a year before he returned to Lu. Three years later, his only son, Kong Li, died too. He was even more distressed by the death of his two students, Yan Hui and Zi Lu. They had been extremely devoted to him and had followed him for 14 years during his journey through ten states, sharing all his hardships and difficulties. Yan Hui died of illness in poverty; Zi Lu was an important official in the state of Wei after his master returned to Lu, and was killed in a coup within the court.

In 479 B.C. Confucius fell ill. One day he stood at his door, clutching a walking stick in his hand, and said to himself, "Mount Tai may collapse! House beams may decay! Wise men may wither!" Seven days later he died at he age of 73.*

------

* Traditionally the Chinese say that one is one year old in the year of one's birth, and two years old the next year. So Confucius (551-479 B.C.) was 73 years old when he died.

第二章 孔子生平

　　春秋时期一百个左右的邦国中有一个鲁国,位于强大的齐国南边, 在今山东省南部。鲁虽然弱小, 但享有光荣的文化传统。西周建立之初, 鲁为周公旦的封地。因为他留在镐京辅佐年幼的成王执政, 他的长子伯禽, 作为他的继承人, 便去治理鲁国。伯禽带去许多典章文物,在那里推行他父亲制定的仪礼及其他制度。在五百年后的春秋时期, 这些仪礼在诸侯的纷争及社会的变革中受到破坏, 但在鲁国却保留了一些。

　　孔子的祖先原为鲁国的邻国宋国的贵族。后来有一人卷入朝廷的权力斗争而被杀,他的儿子逃到鲁国去避祸,就在鲁定居下来。此人的后代中有一位武士

（贵族中的最低一级）叫叔梁纥。其实他姓孔，名纥，字叔梁。

叔梁纥结过两次婚，生了几个女儿和一个跛足的儿子。当时的习俗使女儿做不了继承人，而让跛足的儿子继承又不甚光彩，所以他在六十多岁时又结了一次婚。妻子很年轻，名叫颜徵在。婚后不久，她生了一个儿子。其时为鲁襄公二十二年，或公元前551年。儿子取名孔丘，字仲尼。据传他的父母在他出生前曾去附近的尼丘山祈祷山神，保佑他们得子，因而用尼与丘为儿子命名。

孔子三岁时，父亲去世。母亲带他从父亲原来住的地方陬邑迁到鲁国都城曲阜。在曲阜，母子二人生活相当艰难。因为孔子从小就对学习表现出极大的兴趣，母亲尽可能帮助他、鼓励他，甚至为他准备祭祀用品，让他学会有关的仪礼。可惜年轻的寡母没有能活到看见儿子成为有名的学者，在他只有十六、七岁时便去世了。

孑然一身的少年孔子，一方面孜孜不倦地学习，一方面设法养活他自己。后来他回忆这一段生活的时候说，"吾十有五而志于学；"（2. 4）*又说："吾少也贱，故多能鄙事。"（9. 6）他没有提过那时做些什

---

*即《论语》第二篇第四章。以下凡引自《论语》的语录皆在括号内注明篇、章数。

么"鄙事",据别的书上说,他替办丧事的人家吹过喇叭,管过牛羊,还管过仓库。

在鲁国的丰富的文化遗产熏陶中成长的孔子,勤奋好学,逐渐使自己有了名声,在贵族中也有了相应的地位。大概在十九岁时他结了婚,次年生了一个儿子。当时鲁国的统治者鲁昭公还送了一条鲤鱼表示庆贺。孔子认为这是一件光荣的事,就以鲤为儿子的名,以伯鱼为他的字。

在那个时候,每一个士都该掌握好六种知识或本领:礼、乐、射、御、书、数,统称"六艺"。礼是贵族行为的准则和多种仪式;乐是贵族的一种文化修养,也是多种典礼的伴奏;射指射箭的技术;御指驾马车的技术;书就是写字;数就是计算。孔子主要通过自学,掌握了六艺。在自学的同时,他也不放过任何可以请教别人的机会。《论语》记载:"子入太庙,每事问。"(3.15)就是证明。

孔子并深入研究六种典籍,即《诗》(古代诗集,其中有民歌,也有多种典礼所用的歌词)、《书》(古代历史文件)、《礼》(多种礼节及仪式的规范)、《乐》(古代乐曲)、《易》(对六十四卦的阐释,其中包括一些哲理)、《春秋》(一部编年史)。这六部典籍曾经也称"六艺",到汉代以后则称"六经"。

孔子说自己"三十而立"(2.4),大概是说到三十岁左右他已经对多种知识和多种典籍进行了系统的研究，并形成了自己对历史、社会和人类的观点。也就是说，他已经有了自己的信念或哲学，此后的主要目标是把它付之实践，予以推广，给在黑暗中摸索的人带来光明。

他采用的主要途径是教育。对慕名而来求教的人，他都予以指导。实际上他办了一个私立学校。这件事有重大的历史意义，在教育史上具有划时代性。在孔子以前，教育和政府职位一样，被贵族所垄断。贵族子弟可以在政府办的特殊学校学习，准备做官。这种学校的大门对老百姓是永远关着的。孔子是中国历史上打破这种垄断的第一个人。他把教育带给所有的人，尤其是非贵族出身的人。

从他三十岁左右以学问渊博闻名起，直到他七十三岁去世时止，他的教学活动从未停止过。据说他一生中共教了三千个学生，其中七十二人精通六经，在学术、政治及其他方面有突出的成就。

他的影响随着学生人数的增加而越来越大。鲁国的统治者终于认识到起用他来治理国家是合适的，在他五十一岁时任命他为中都宰，就是中都县长。大概做得不错，很快就提升为大司寇，相当于现在的公安局长，这个职务他担任了三年左右。

在这期间，鲁国国君与强大的齐国的国君有一次会见。孔子深知仪礼，所以鲁国国君请他任相礼（类似司仪），参与这次会见。齐国国君原来打算威胁鲁君，使他服从自己的意志。孔子觉察到齐君的谋划，机智而勇敢地处理当时出现的情势，挫败了齐君的意图。

这次外交斗争的胜利给孔子带来了声誉，使鲁国的统治者更加信任他，要他行摄相事，与闻国政，也就是负责政府的实际工作。他治国很有成绩，鲁国成为一个平静的、有秩序的国家。《史记》上说鲁国当时卖肉的不敢要虚价，男女分开走在路上，在路上丢失的东西没人捡，外地人到鲁国像回到家里一样。

但孔子与掌权的贵族之间有严重的政治分歧。当时鲁国国君鲁定公并无实权，实权落在三家贵族及他们的家属手中。孔子一向主张忠君尊王，对这种形势十分不满，于是着手消除贵族的权力，这当然引起贵族的反对。这时齐国又给鲁国的执政者季桓子送来八十名能歌善舞的美女，使得他无心处理政事。在此形势下，孔子觉得治国的主张无法实现，便决定离开。这一年他五十五岁。

他开始了一个访问约十个邦国，历时十四年的行程。在几个忠实的学生陪同下，他从一国到另一国，先后与六个国君谈他的仁政主张，希望得到任用，有机会把他的理想付之实践。但在这些邦国里，他不是被冷落，就是被有礼貌地闲置。他和随行的人不止一次地遭遇到极大的困难，生病挨饿，甚至有生命危险。当他听说有人描写他像一个"丧家之狗"时，他笑着说:"然哉,然哉!"*但不管发生什么情况,他都乐观、坦然,继续对弟子施教,带弟子演习礼仪,朗诵诗文,弹琴唱歌。

这期间,在鲁国掌权的老一代贵族已经死去,新的一代控制了朝政。孔子的一些学生已成为重要官员,在他们劝说下,这些新上台的掌权者派人到孔子当时居留的卫国去迎接他回鲁。孔子同意了,这样便回到鲁国,该年他六十八岁。

孔子对奔波十四年而没有实现理想固然感到失望,但其实这个失败是不可避免的。在那个战争与并吞经常发生的时期,各国统治者自然是急于使本国富强起来。孔子所宣扬的仁政对他们来说一定是太不实际了,不可能引起他们认真的考虑。

回到鲁国后,孔子不再担任政府职务,而是致力于教育和经典的整理。

孔子很可能用六经为教材。他在最后的几年中,对这六部书进行了整理和修订,去伪存真,去芜存菁,使它们趋于完善。

孔子自己没有著作。在他那个时候,个人写书和出版书还没有成为惯例。他所整理的古籍都是西周或更早时候传下来的朝廷文件和历史纪录,或专门搜集的民歌。除少数例外,都没有作者的姓名。再者,孔

---

*见《史记》"孔子世家"。

子本人愿意述旧而不愿创新。他说他"述而不作,信而好古。"(7.1)

幸而有一本书比六经更为直接、更为清楚地表达了孔子的观点和理论——《论语》。这本书汇集了孔子和他的主要门徒的评论、答问、谈话约五百条,共一万二千七百字,显然是由那些听到孔子谈话和听到门徒们讨论孔子教诲的学生们记录、整理的。这五百条语录涉及到许多方面的极为重要的问题,诸如仁和礼,政和法,教育和知识,音乐和诗歌,君子和小人,等等,还包括一些有关孔子的生活习惯、作风、性格的简略的描述。

孔子整理的六经和这本《论语》,除《乐经》外,在秦始皇焚书之后幸存下来,从汉以后,成为历代学者学习和研究的主要典籍,影响极为深远。它们,尤其是《论语》,包涵不可估量的智慧,像火炬一样照亮中国人的道路达两千年之久,直到本世纪初情况才有所改变。

孔子晚年遭遇到一系列的不幸。他的妻子在他回鲁前一年去世。三年后,他的独生子,孔鲤,也死了。他的两个门徒,颜回和子路之死使他十分悲痛。这两个学生对他极为忠诚,曾经陪伴他访问十国,和他一起度过了那艰难的十四年。颜回死于贫病;子路于孔子回鲁后在卫国任职,在一次宫廷政变中被杀害。

公元前479年孔子患病。一天他扶着手杖站在家门口说:"泰山其颓乎!梁木其坏乎!哲人其萎乎!"
七天后去世,享年七十三岁。

Chapter Three: Confucius and the Way

Confucius said, "If I learned the Way in the morning, I would die content in the evening." (4.8) This saying reveals his love for and his eagerness to seek the truth. He spent all his life exploring, spreading, and promoting the Way. To him the Way was life, the only thing that mattered.

In modern terminology, the Way means the truth, or objective law, or correct thinking. Confucius put forward a series of theories about life, society, and government which formed an integral whole. Some of them, as we view them today, 2,500 years after they were formulated, are no doubt outdated; but the main part or essence of his Way is still valuable and valid, and can be taken as ideals and objectives for which mankind should strive.

Firstly, he pointed out the supreme importance of morality. In Chinese intellectual history Confucius was the first to regard morality as the first and most important requirement of a man and a ruler. He explained what moral qualities one should have and what moral standard one should attain, and made it clear that everyone could develop their moral character, if they so desired, for it was not something that one could not reach for.

Secondly, he had clearly-formulated and exact views about government. The prince or ruler of a state should, he believed, be an upright man with a sound moral character, one who believed in humane government and the necessity of enriching and educating the populace. He was opposed to harsh laws and severe punishments, and hated war. These views were not accepted by any ruler of the day, but the fact that he proclaimed them showed his far-sightedness and adherence to sound principles.

Thirdly, he had many valuable ideas about educational principles and teaching methods. His life-long teaching experience was guided by and also enriched his theories of education. Many of them are still valid today; some of his methods are even practicable.

Fourthly, in connection with man's relations with Heaven, interpersonal relations, and ways of thinking, he also had his own views. The mean, for instance, reflects a basic law of nature and human society.

The following chapters will discuss these four aspects of Confucius' thought. Although he treated other subjects, these four embrace his main theories, especially those that have exerted tremendous influence on Chinese culture and Chinese thought.

To understand and study Confucius' thought one had best use as the key text *The Analects*, which contains his own words and is of course more reliable than other people's explanations and comments. Such classical works as *The Great Learning*, *The Doctrine of the Mean*, and *The Mencius**

---

* *The Great Learning* and *The Doctrine of the Mean* are originally two articles collected in *Records of Rites*, compiled by Dai Sheng of the Western Han. It was said that *The Great Learning* was written by Zeng Shen, a disciple of Confucius, and *The Doctrine of the Mean* by Zi Si, Confucius' grandson. The two articles contain a few similar views: both stress the importance of self-cultivation and loyalty and reciprocity, and both value sincerity. *The Mencius* was written by Mencius (c. 372-289 B.C.) and Wan Zhang and other disciples of his. The book expounds some of Confucius' views. Zhu Xi (1130-1200), a prominent scholar of the Southern Song, put the above three books and *The Analects* together and called them *The Four Books*, which were to be the main Confucian classics studied by all scholars for about 800 years.

are worth reading too, since they interpret
Confucius' thought and may verify and clarify
certain points in *The Analects*.

第三章 孔子与道

孔子说:"朝闻道,夕死可矣。"(4. 8)(早晨听到真理,就是晚上死去也可以。)这句话表达了他追求真理、热爱真理的心情。他一生都在探索道,传布道,推行道。道对他来说就是生命,就是一切。

用我们今天的说法,道是指真理、客观规律,或正确思想。孔子提出了许多关于人生、社会和政治的主张,并且形成了一个完整的体系。在两千五百年后的今天看起来,其中一部分无疑已经过时;但就其主体看,他的道仍然有价值、站得住,仍然可以看作人类的美好的理想和奋斗的目标。

首先,他强调道德的重大意义。在中国思想史上,孔子是第一个把道德作为做人和治国的首要条件提出来的哲人。他阐明道德的内容和标准，还进一步指出，每个人都可以通过自己的努力来提高道德修养，道德并不是高不可攀的。

其次，他对治国之道有一系列明确的论述。他认为一国之君或统治者必须是正直的有道德的人。对人民必须实行仁政，使他们富裕，并对他们进行教育。他反对严刑峻法，反对战争。他的主张没有被当时的任何统治者采纳，但表现出他的远见卓识，和不寻常的坚持原则的精神。

第三，他在教育原则和教学方法方面，提出了非常精辟的见解。他多年的教学实践和他关于教育和教学法的主张是互相结合、互相促进的。这些主张，在今天看来，仍然极有参考价值，有的完全可以采用。

第四，他在天人关系、人际关系、思想方法等方面，也提出了自己的看法。例如中庸便反映了自然界和人类社会的一条根本规律。

我们将从上述四个方面来介绍孔子的思想。他还讨论过其他一些问题，但这四个方面大体上可以概括他的主要观点，尤其是对中国文化和中国人的思想有极大影响的观点。

了解和研究孔子思想，宜从《论语》入手，并以这本书为依据。它记载了孔子自己说的话，比别人的转述或评介更为可靠。其他解释孔子思想的古籍，如

《大学》、《中庸》、《孟子》*等书，也有印证的作用和参考的价值。

---

*《大学》和《中庸》原是西汉戴圣编辑的《礼记》中的两篇论文。相传《大学》为孔子门徒曾参所作，《中庸》为孔子孙子思所作。两文的思想有许多一致的地方，都强调修身和忠恕之道，重视诚的作用。《孟子》为战国时孟轲（约前372—289）及其门徒万章等人所作，阐述孔子的某些思想。南宋的朱熹（1130—1200）把《大学》、《中庸》、《论语》、《孟子》编为《四书》，使它们成为以后的八百年中儒家最重要的经典。

Chapter Four: On Morality

Confucius placed great emphasis on morality. Most of his sayings recorded in *The Analects* concern moral questions. Of all moral qualities humanity or humaneness is the one he specially emphasized — it constituted for him the core of moral character.

Why did Confucius lay so much emphasis on moral character with humanity as its core? To understand this we have to recall how, in those days, man regraded his own position and destiny.

In the highly stratified society of the day, the common people believed that they were born to be ruled by the king and his vassals, to do hard work and endure a hard life, to serve their masters as slaves, serfs, or servants. They had to accept this fate, they believed, because it was decided by Heaven, which, though intangible, had control over everything, and which no one had the right to question, let alone disobey.

Besides obeying the will of Heaven, people had to respect their ancestors, who in their graves had the power to protect and punish their living descendants. Funerals and memorial rituals in honor of ancestors were very important and had to be conducted in earnest and with solemnity, for they affected the fortunes or misfortunes of the living.

Then there were ghosts and spirits. These should not be offended, for they also affected the destiny of the living. Although they were invisible, they were believed to lurk in the dark and to be capable of doing harm to people.

Therefore the common people lived under threefold control: that of Heaven above the earth; that of ancestors, ghosts and spirits beneath it; and that of the rulers of the earth.

The rulers, the king and all the tiers of vassals below him, believed that they were born to rule. This power was given them by Heaven, which brooked no query. The rites were the only rules they had to observe.

During the Spring and Autumn Period, as a result of social and political upheavals, all the traditional institutions and concepts, such as the rites and the will of Heaven, failed to check the ambitious and greedy rulers, and the misery of the common people was intensified by the incessant wars.

Confucius came to the fore, determined to save mankind from this tragic condition by means of reason. He did not emphasize the futility of resisting the will of Heaven, nor did he stress the danger of disobeying ancestors, ghosts and spirits. He did not advocate trying to eradicate war by waging war, or employing the law to curb man's wrong-doing. Instead, he endeavored to find a fundamental solution, a solution that would forever change men's thinking — to awaken all people to a realization of the nature of man, of the right way to be a man. It was for this purpose that he expounded the meaning of humanity and other virtues.

第四章 论德

　　孔子对道德极为重视。《论语》记载的他的谈话，绝大多数是讨论道德或与道德有关的问题。在各种道德中，他特别强调仁，仁在他看来是道德的核心。

　　为什么孔子如此重视以仁为核心的道德呢？为了理解这一点，还得回顾一下在他那个时代人怎样看待自己的地位和命运。

　　在那个社会等级分明的时代，老百姓（庶民）认为他们生下来就该受到王、公、侯等多级贵族的统治，必须艰苦劳动，只能过艰难的日子，当奴隶、农奴，或仆人来伺候主人。他们必须接受这样的命运，因为这是天命。天命虽然看不见、摸不着，但控制一切，不容怀疑，更不能反抗。

除了服从天命之外，人人还得尊敬祖先。祖先在坟墓里仍然可以保佑或惩罚活着的后代。所以丧事和祭祀十分重要，必须认真、隆重地举行，因为这影响活着的人的命运。

还有鬼神也是不能得罪的，也与活人的吉凶有关。尽管谁也没有看到过鬼神，但人们相信他们藏在暗处，可以对人造成损害。

所以老百姓受到三重控制：上面的天，地下的祖先及鬼神，地上的统治者。

统治者，由君王到多级贵族，相信他们是生下来统治老百姓的，这是上天授予他们的权力，不容怀疑和动摇。他们只要遵守礼的约束就行了。

但在春秋时期，由于政治和社会的动荡，原有的制度和观念，包括礼、天命等等，不再能约束有野心的、贪得无厌的贵族；而老百姓的命运，则被频繁的战争弄得更加悲惨。

这时孔子站出来，要用理性挽救人类。他不强调天命之不可违，更不宣扬祖先及鬼神的不可抗。他不主张用战争来消灭战争，或用法制来压服人们。相反，他试图从思想认识上，或者说从根本上，来解决问题。他努力唤醒所有的人来看清人类的本质，理解怎样做人才是正确的。这就是他阐明仁及其他道德的意义的目的所在。

Man and Humanity

"To be humane is to be a man,"* said Confucius. This saying may be construed as meaning that humanity is the fundamental quality of man, or that humanity is the nature of man. It is this nature that makes a man a man. To put it in a negative way, a man without this nature ceases to be a man, for he is not fundamentally different from other animals.

As man has a moral nature, to adhere to moral principles should be everyone's first consideration. Moral principles are more important than all other things, including position, wealth, even life. Confucius said,

Wealth and high position are desired by all men, but I would not have them if they were not won in the right way. Poverty and low position are hated by all men, but I would not leave them if they could not be rid of in the right way. How could a gentleman make a name if he departed from humanity? A

*See *The Docrtine of the Mean.*

gentleman never departs from humanity, not even during the short space of a meal, not even when he is in a great haste, or when he is wandering from place to place away from home.(4.5)

Confucius pointed out here with great emphasis that under no circumstances and at no time should one depart from humanity, or, in other words, moral principles. Humanity is the fundamental virtue; it stands for all the good qualities that man could and should have. Confucius gave very clear explanations of the meaning of humanity:

Fan Chi asked about humanity. Confucius said, "Love other men." (12.22)

A humane man helps others to stand up when he wants to stand up himself, and helps others to understand things when he wants to understand things himself. (6.30)

Zhong Gong asked about humanity. Confucius said, "When you are outside of your home, behave as though you were meeting important guests; when you are using the common people's labor, behave as though you were conducting a solemn sacrificial ceremony. Do not impose on others what you do not desire yourself. Bear no ill will towards the state or noble family

where you work." (12.2)

"Love other men" expresses most succinctly the Confucian essence of humanity. "Men" here is not qualified by any word, so it refers to all men, whether they are privileged or humble, rich or poor, old or young, near or far. On another occasion, Confucius said, "Love the people extensively," (1.6) a sentiment similar to that of "love other men." One who loves other men will naturally do things that are beneficial to the people. How wonderful the world would be if all people would love other men! But there has never been such a time. There are always people who do not love other men and will do major or minor things harmful to others. Obviously one way to deal with such people is to enforce the law, but a more enduring and effective solution lies in raising people's moral standards.

Confucius himself loved other men. At a time when social classes were distinct, he upheld the principle of "teaching everyone without making distinctions," and accepted as students people from all levels of society, giving them instruction without favoring one over another. Yan Hui, for instance, though a poor man, was the student he praised most highly.

To help others stand up when one wants to stand up oneself, and to help others to understand things when one wants to understand things oneself – this explains how one may love others in an active way. To stand up means to be established or successful; to understand things means to understand the truth. A humane man would not be happy if he alone is successful or able to understand the truth while others are not. He feels obliged to help others to succeed or comprehend like himself. Confucius was "never tired of learning or teaching," (7.2) and this exemplifies his spirit of humanity. Mencius said, "Whenever he saw someone drowning, Yu felt as if he had been the cause; whenever he saw someone hungry, Ji felt as if he had been the cause."* He who has this feeling is a humane man.

In the third quotation above, the main idea is not to impose on others what one does not desire oneself. This explains how one may love others in a passive way: when it is impossible to help others to succeed or understand, the very least one should do is not to hurt others.

The active and passive side of humanity may be captured in these two ideas: loyalty and reciprocity. Confucius said, "Be loyal to others;" (13.19) and "Can you be loyal to someone without teaching him?"

---

*See The Mencius, 8.29. Ji was a legendary hero who taught people to plant certain crops.

(14.7) Zeng Shen, a well-known disciple of his, said that he examined himself three times every day, and the first question he asked himself was whether he was loyal in dealing with others.

These axioms are in keeping with the spirit of helping others to stand up and to understand things. Loyalty also means being faithful to one's prince. When explaining the correct relationship between prince and minister, Confucius said, "The prince should employ his ministers according to the rites; the ministers should serve their prince with loyalty." (3.19)

On the meaning of reciprocity, Confucius gave an explanation himself:

> **Zi Gong asked, "Is there a word that one can practice all one's life?" Confucius said, "Perhaps *reciprocity* is such a word. Do not impose on others what you do not desire yourself." (15.24)**

So reciprocity means that one should not impose on others what one does not desire oneself, and this is something that one should do all one's life.

About the supreme importance of loyalty and reciprocity, Zeng Shen made a famous comment:

> **Confucius said, "Shen, there is one thread that runs through my Way." "Yes," Zeng Shen answered. Then the master went out. Other**

**students asked, "What did he mean?" Zeng
Shen said, "The master's Way can be
summed up in two words: loyalty and
reciprocity." (4.15)**

Zeng Shen's generalization may not cover all
aspects of Confucius' philosophy, but it gets close
to its essence. Loyalty and reciprocity, as
expressions of humanity, are norms of action guided
by humanity, which is at the very core of Confucius'
thought.

Humanity is the supreme principle. To realize it,
one should if necessary surrender everything else,
including life itself.

**A determined or humane man never gives
up humanity to save his life, but he may
sacrifice his life to realize humanity.(15.9)**

A humane man is always open and above board,
never doing anything he might regret, free from
worries and fears, at peace with himself and the
world. This state of mind is not illusory, but
attainable. Confucius said,

**Is humanity far away? It will come to me if
I desire it. (7.30)**

"I desire it" implies making an effort, in keeping with
the following injunction:

**To practice humanity depends on oneself.
Can it depend on anyone else? (12.1)**

The Chinese character 仁 is made up of 人 and 二. This, according to certain scholars, indicates that humanity is necessary wherever and whenever two persons are together or, in other words, when there is contact between people. No one can live alone, isolated from other men; therefore a humane spirit is indispensable for all people. In living and working together, people should be helpful and cooperative, respectful and friendly to each other, so that there is warmth and harmony. Only when people are like this is it possible for there to be social progress, peace and happiness.

By putting forward his philosophy of humanity Confucius aimed to free man from traditional superstition, political ambitions, material greed, and all sorts of spiritual shackles. He gave human life a meaning and purpose. He set a goal for which all men could strive. So his advancement of the theory of humanity means the discovery of the meaning of human life, or the value of man.

人与仁

孔子说:"仁者人也。"* 这句话可以理解为仁是人类的最基本的品质,或者说仁是人类的本质。正是这个品质使人成其为人;反过来说,没有这个品质,人就不成其为人,就和其他动物没有本质上的差别了。

因为人具有仁或道德的本质,做人首先要坚持道德的原则。这个原则是压倒一切的,比任何别的东西,比地位、财富,甚至比生命都更为重要。孔子说:

> 富与贵,是人之所欲也;不以其道,得之不处也。贫与贱,是人之所以恶也;不以其道,得之不去也。君子去仁,恶乎成名?君子无终食之间违仁,造次必于是,颠沛必于是。(4.5)
>
> (财富与尊贵是人们想要的,但不用正当的方法,得到了也是不能要的。贫穷与下贱是人们所厌恶的,但不用正当的方 法,即使贫贱也不摆脱。君子离开仁怎么能有君子的名声呢?君子不会在一顿饭的短时间内离开仁,就是在匆忙 的时候也不离开仁,就是在困难的时候也不离开仁。)

孔子在这里着重指出:不论在什么情况下,不论

---

* 见《中庸》。

在什么时候，人都不能离开仁，也就是不能离开道德
的原则。仁是最根本的道德，代表人所能有的或应该
有的一切好的品质。孔子对仁的涵义有明确的解释：

　　樊迟问仁。子曰："爱人。"(12. 22)
　　夫仁者，己欲立而立人，己欲达而达人。(6. 30)
　　仲弓问仁。子曰："出门如见大宾，使民如承大
　　祭。己所不欲，勿施于人。在邦无怨，在家无
　　怨。"(12. 2)
　　(仲弓问仁的意思。孔子说："出外活动好像去见
　　贵宾，使用老百姓好像在进行祭祀。自己不想要
　　的事物，就不要强加给别人。对于邦国或家族都
　　没有怨恨。)

　　"爱人"二字非常简明地说出了"仁"的实质。这
里的"人"字没有加任何限定词，可以认为是指一切
人，不分尊卑、贫富、长幼、远近。在另一场合，孔
子说"泛爱众"(1. 6)：广泛地爱大众，或者说博爱，
和这里说的"爱人"应该是同样的意思。一个人有爱
人的心，自然会做有益于大众的事。如果人人都有爱
人的心，那世界将是多么美好！可惜从来就没有这样
的时候。任何时候都有大大小小的不爱人的人，在干
大大小小的损人、害人的事。他们之中权力小的会损
害个别人，权力大的会损害千万人。加强法制当然是
解决这个问题的一个途径，但法制并不能解决全部问
题。有些国家的法律订得十分周密，法院的工作也很
有效率，但坏事仍层出不穷。更为根本的办法应该是

普及道德教育，加强所有的人的道德观念，使人人都
有爱人的思想。

孔子本人树立了爱人的榜样。在那社会等级分明
的时代，他主张"有教无类"（15.39)，接受各阶层
出身的人为学生，对他们一视同仁地给予指导。他最
赞扬的学生颜回就是一个穷苦的青年。

"己欲立而立人，己欲达而达人"是从积极的意
义上说明如何爱人。"立"表示站得住，或事业上有
成就；"达"表示通达，也就是懂得道理。只是自己
有成就、懂得许多道理，对于仁者来说，还是不够
的；还应该帮助别人有成就、懂得道理。*孔子"学
而不厌，诲人不倦"就是这种思想的体现。孟子说：
"禹思天下有溺者，由己溺之也；稷思天下有饥者，由
己饥之也"**也表现了这种思想：别人溺水就好像是
自己使他溺水，别人饥饿就好像是自己使他饥饿。有
这种感觉的人便是仁者。

上面第三条语录的重点是"己所不欲，勿施于
人"八个字。这是从消极的意义上说明如何爱人：如
果不能帮助别人立和达，至少不要损害别人。

这积极和消极两个方面，可用"忠"和"恕"两
个词来概括。孔子说："与人忠。"（13.19）还说："忠

---

* 另一种解释是自己想做事成功，也要帮助别人做事成功。
** 《孟子》8.29。

焉，能勿诲乎？"（14．7）（对一个人忠实，能不教
诲他吗？）他的著名弟子之一曾参说："吾日三省吾
身"（我每天三次检查自己），其中的第一条是"为人
谋而不忠乎？"（1．4）

这些说法和"立人"、"达人"的精神是一致的。
"忠"的意思还包括忠于君主。孔子在阐明君臣关系
时说："君使臣以礼，臣事君以忠。"（3．19）（君应
该按照礼的规定使用臣，臣应该忠诚地为君服务。）

对于"恕"，孔子自己做过解释。

　　子贡曰："有一言而可以终身行之者乎？"
　　子曰："其恕乎！己所不欲，勿施于人。"（15.24）

恕就是己所不欲，勿施于人，这条原则是可以终
身奉行的。

关于忠和恕的极端重要性，曾参有句名言：

　　子曰：参乎！吾道一以贯之。"曾子曰："唯。"子
　　出，门人问曰："何谓也？"曾子曰："夫子之道，
　　忠恕而已矣。"（4．15）

　　（孔子说"参呀！我的学说有一个基本概念贯穿
　　着。"曾子说："是。"孔子走出去，其他学生问
　　曾子："什么意思？"曾子说："他老先生的学说
　　就是忠和恕。"）

曾子把老师的学说概括为忠恕，也许不够全面，
但是抓住了实质。忠和恕是仁的表现，是以仁为指导
思想的行动准则，而仁是孔子思想的核心。

仁是至高无上的原则。为了仁的实现，在必要

时，一切别的东西，包括生命，都可以牺牲：

> 志士仁人，无求生以害仁，有杀身以成仁。(15.
> 9)

一个高尚的仁人，襟怀坦白，无愧于人，不忧不惧，内心平静。这种境界不是空想，而是可以达到的：

> 仁远乎哉？我欲仁，斯仁至矣。(7. 30)
>
> (仁离我很远吗？我要仁，仁就来了。)

"我欲仁"就是做出主观努力，所以孔子又说：

> 为仁由己，而由人乎哉？ (12. 1)
>
> (实践仁全靠自己，难道能靠别人吗？)

有的学者认为，"仁"字是"人"和"二"组成的，这表示只要有两个人在一起，也就是在发生人际关系的时候，仁便是必要的。任何人都不应离开人群，单独生活。在互相交往中，人都应有仁的精神；互助合作，互敬互爱，温暖和谐。只有这样，社会才能进步，才会有和平与幸福。

这样，孔子把人从传统的迷信、政治野心、物质欲望，及多种精神束缚中解放出来，赋予人的生活以意义和目的，树立一个人人可以争取达到的目标。所以仁的提出意味着人生意义的发现，也是人的价值的发现。

Rightness, Propriety, Wisdom and Trustworthiness

Starting from humanity and in connection with it, Confucius identified many other virtues in the hope that all people, especially those of the upper classes, might cultivate and practice them. They include: rightness, propriety, loyalty, reciprocity, trustworthiness, respectfulness, reverence, wisdom, courage, filial piety, brotherly love, resoluteness, perseverance, simplicity, reticence, tolerance, generosity, diligence, kindness, mildness, thrift, politeness, forbearance, peacefulness, uprightness, eagerness in learning, readiness in correcting mistakes, modesty, and the sense of shame. Five of these virtues — humanity, rightness, propriety, wisdom, and trustworthiness — have been singled out as the most fundamental by important Confucian scholars of later ages. As humanity has been discussed in the previous section, this section will deal with the other four.

Rightness. Just as humanity is the essential quality of man, so rightness is the criterion for his conduct and behavior. One should always do, say and think of the right thing. Otherwise one might make mistakes and might go so far as to cause trouble to society and the state.

Zi Lu asked, "Does the gentleman consider courage a high virtue?" Confucius said, "The gentleman puts rightness before courage. A gentleman who has courage but does not know rightness will become a trouble maker, and a small man who has courage and does not know rightness will become a brigand." (17.23)

The opposite of rightness is profit or gain. Confucius mentioned these opposites side by side to caution his disciples against treating them in the wrong way:

The gentleman knows what is right; the small man knows what is profitable. (4.16)

A gentleman...thinks of rightness at the sight of gain. (16.10)

A complete man...thinks of rightness when he sees profit. (14.12)

These sayings show that Confucius put rightness before gain; he valued rightness and disparaged gain. But he was not against the common people seeking profit. When he was enlightening a disciple on the way of government, he said that it was good to "benefit the common people where they can be benefited." (20.2) Many later Confucianists, however, tended to exclude profit or gain from consideration, thinking that the pursuit of profit or gain would only lead people astray. This differs from Confucius' view on the question.

Propriety. Propriety means the observance of the rites. The rites meant not what we call good manners today, but rather ceremonies, institutions, customs, norms, and rules of behavior. They were devised to guide and restrain relations among people, especially people of the upper classes. There were rules, for instance, about how a prince should treat his ministers and how a son should treat his father. Like unwritten laws, the rites meant to ensure social order and stability.

Confucius attached great importance to the rites. Most, if not all, social ills of his day, such as vassals not obeying the king, assistants not obeying their masters, perpetual warfare, and the frequency of usurpations, he attributed to the collapse of the rites. In his view the only way to halt these was through a restoration of the rites.

Duke Jing asked Confucius about government. Confucius answered, "The prince should behave like a prince, the minister like a minister, the father father, and the son son." (12.11)

It is obvious that Confucius meant, when giving his answer, that all people — princes and ministers, fathers and sons — should behave in accordance with the rites, for only then could a state be well governed.

On other occasions, Confucius spoke frequently about the significance of the rites:

> **If not guided by the rites, one would be exhausted when trying to be respectful, cowardly when trying to be cautious, dangerous when trying to be courageous, and bitter when trying to be outspoken. (18.2)**

> **When those above observe the rites, the common people will be easy to command. (14.41)**

So in Confucius' view, good qualities like respectfulness, cautiousness, courage, and outspokenness may become weaknesses and lead to mistakes if they are not guided by the rites, and the rites are indispensable to those who want to govern their states well.

Moreover, according to Confucius, the rites are inseparable from humanity.

> **Yan Yuan asked about humanity. Confucius said, "Humanity means to restrain oneself and conform to the rites..." Yan Yuan said, "May I ask about the specific requirements?"**

Confucius said, "Do not look if it does not conform to the rites; do not listen if it does not conform to the rites; do not speak if it does not conform to the rites; do not act if it does not conform to the rites." Yan Yuan said, "Although I am not bright, I will follow these instructions." (12.1)

Why is self-restraint and conformity to the rites equivalent to humanity? One possible explanation follows. To restrain oneself is to overcome selfishness and put other people's interests before one's own; to conform to the rites is to do what is right; thinking and acting in this way reflects humanity. In other words, only a humane man can restrain himself and conform to the rites. It can therefore be said that humanity and the rites are two sides of the same coin: humanity is the inside and the rites the outside; humanity is the content and the rites the form.

It follows that a man who is not humane has no use for the rites, so Confucius said,

What use are the rites to a man who is not humane? What use is music to a man who is not humane? (13.3)

The effect of music is similar to that of the rites, for both aim at harmony, a principle which is desired only by humane men.

Wisdom. It was considered a virtue because it mainly meant the understanding of the Way, and this understanding was a prerequisite of following the Way.

To Confucius the knowledge of nature and that of farming and manufacturing were not important. What was important was the way to be a man and the way to govern a state. So he said,

> **The gentleman is after the Way, not food...**
> **The gentleman worries about the Way, not**
> **about poverty. (15.32)**

Fan Chi, one of his students, asked him how to grow crops and vegetables. He said that he did not know these things as well as an old farmer did. Then he continued,

> **When those above love the rites, the**
> **common people will not dare to be**
> **disrespectful; when those above love**
> **rightness, the common people will not dare**
> **to be disobedient; when those above love**
> **trustworthiness, the common people will not**
> **dare to be dishonest. If things are like this,**
> **common people from the four directions will**
> **come with their children carried on their**
> **backs. What need is there to learn to grow**
> **crops? (13.4)**

This saying shows that Confucius expected his

students to understand the meaning of the rites, rightness, trustworthiness and other virtues, rather than to learn to do specific things like growing crops.

In a saying of Zi Xia, one of his well-known disciples, the connection between wisdom and humanity is established:

There is humanity in learning extensively, persevering in one's aims, inquiring about familiar things, and examining matters close to oneself. (19.6)

According to Zi Xia, to learn extensively for the purpose of self-cultivation and an understanding of life would certainly give one wisdom, and this wisdom would help to improve one's moral character. Without such wisdom, one would be like a blind man, unable to distinguish between right and wrong, let alone govern a state. A state under wise and humane men might be well governed, its common people might live and work in peace, and then agriculture and handicrafts would develop and prosper. Confucius criticized Fan Chi wishing to learn to grow crops, just because he failed to see what should be given priority.

Confucius praised both wise men and humane men:

The wise enjoy water; the humane enjoy mountains. The wise are active; the humane

are serene. The wise are happy; the humane have a long life. (6.23)

The wise are free from puzzles; the humane are free from worries; the brave are free from fears. (9.29)

Trustworthiness. The last of the five virtues, trustworthiness subsumes in its meaning trust, faithfulness, and sincerity. Without it normal relations between men, including relations between superiors and subordinates, would be impossible. About this virtue Confucius said,

I do not know how a man who has lost trustworthiness can function as a man. How can a big cart move forward if it has lost a pin in the yoke-bar, or a small cart move forward if it has lost a pin in the collar-bar? (2.22)

The pins of the yoke-bar and collar-bar are both crucial parts of carts, for they connect the yoke to the cart. Without them the horse or the cattle cannot be harnessed and consequently the cart cannot move. Similarly, trustworthiness is what connects one person with another. The lack of sincerity and faithfulness, equated with trustworthiness, in human relationships leads to the loss of all effective communication among people.

On other occasions Confucius said that a young

man should be "cautious and trustworthy," (1.6) that a ruler should be "serious and trustworthy," (1.5) and that a gentleman should be "trustworthy in talking with friends." (1.7) One thing that Zeng Shen daily examined himself on was whether he was trustworthy in dealings with friends. These aphorisms show that Confucius and his main disciples considered trustworthiness to be a very important virtue.

In his comment on Fan Chi quoted above, Confucius also mentioned that a ruler should uphold the rites, rightness, and trustworthiness, and thus he might earn his subjects' loyalty and obedience. Furthermore, in one of his talks with Zi Gong he additionally stressed the significance of trustworthiness:

> **Zi Gong asked about government. Confucius said, "If there is enough food and enough arms, the common people will have trust in you." Zi Gong then asked, "If it was necessary to give up one of the three things, which should be given up first?" "Give up arms." "If it was necessary to give up one of the remaining two things, which should be given up then?" "Give up food. Since ancient time, death has always befallen man. The common people who trust no one cannot exist." (12.7)**

What Confucius meant in reference to putting trust before food is that the people, led by a government they trust, will eventually overcome temporary difficulties and produce enough food. However, they will be disunited and disorderly, unable to do anything, and even perish altogether, if they simply do not believe in their government.

义、礼、智、信

　　孔子从仁出发，或联系仁，提出许多道德标准，希望人们，尤其是社会的上层，去理解和实践。他谈到过义、礼、忠、恕、信、恭、敬、智、勇、孝、悌、刚、毅、木、讷、宽、敏、惠、温、良、俭、让、忍、和、正、好学、改过、谦逊、行己有耻，等等。后世一些重要的儒家学者曾从这些品德中提出五种最基本的品德，就是人们常说的仁、义、礼、智、信。上面已经解释了仁，这里谈谈义、礼、智、信。

　　正如仁是人的基本品德，义是人的行动和行为的基本准则。义的主要意思是合理、正确。人应该时时做、说、想正确的事，不然便会犯错误，甚至对社会和国家造成损害。

　　　　子路曰："君子尚勇乎？"子曰："君子义以为上。君子有勇而无义为乱，小人有勇而无义为盗。"(17. 23)

　　　　（子路说："君子崇尚勇吗？"孔子说："君子最崇尚义。君子有勇而无义会作乱，小人有勇而无义会成盗匪。"）

　　义的反面是利或得。孔子几次谈到二者的关系，希望他的弟子正确对待：

君子喻于义，小人喻于利。(4．16)

(君子懂得义，小人懂得利。)

见得思义。(16．10)

(在可以得到什么的时候，要想想是否合理。)

见利思义。(14．12)

这些话表明孔子把义放在利的前面，重义轻利。但他并不反对老百姓谋利。在教诲一个弟子如何从政的时候，他说："因民之所利而利之"(20．2)(在人民能得到利益的地方给他们利益)，便是一例。但很多后世的儒家学者倾向于完全排除利得的想法，认为谋利只会把人引入歧途，这和孔子的看法是有差别的。

现在谈礼。礼主要不是指我们现在常说的礼貌，而是指多种仪式、制度、风俗、常规，及行为的规范。这一切都是为了指导和约束人际关系，首先是上层人士之间的关系。例如君应当怎样对待臣，子应当怎样对待父，都有一定的规定。礼像是不成文法，保证社会秩序与稳定。

孔子对礼极为重视。春秋时期的多种混乱现象，如诸侯不服从天子，大夫不服从诸侯，攻战不停，篡位成风，在他看来，就是礼的崩溃，必须恢复礼才能杜绝。

齐景公问政于孔子。孔子对曰："君君，臣臣，父父，子子。"(12．11)

(齐景公问孔子如何治理国家。孔子答道："君要

像个君，臣要像个臣，父要像个父，子要像个
子。）

显然，孔子在这样回答的时候，意思是所有的人
——君、臣、父、子——都应该按礼行事；只有这样，
国家才能治理好。

在别的场合，孔子多次讲到礼的意义，例如：

恭而无礼则劳，慎而无礼则葸，勇而无礼则乱，
直而无礼则绞。(8．2)
（端庄而无礼就会疲劳不安，谨慎而无礼就会胆
小怕事，勇敢而无礼就会犯上作乱，直率而无礼
就会说话伤人。）
上好礼，则民易使也。(14.41)
（在上位的人按礼行事，老百姓就容易服从他。）

可以看出，孔子认为，就每个人而言，如果不懂
得礼，则其他优良品质，如恭、慎、勇、直，都会变
为缺点或导致错误。在上位的人更应该按礼行事，因
为这有助于治理国家。

孔子还认为礼与仁是分不开的：

颜渊问仁。子曰："克己复礼为仁。……"颜渊
曰："请问其目。"子曰："非礼勿视，非礼勿听，
非礼勿言，非礼勿动。"颜渊曰："回虽不敏，请
事斯语矣。"(12．1)
（颜渊问仁。孔子说："约束自己来实行礼就是
仁。……"颜渊说："请问具体的要求。"孔子说：
"不符合礼的就不看，不符合礼的就不听，不符
合礼的就不说，不符合礼的就不做。"颜渊说：

"我虽然迟钝，但愿努力照这些话去做。")

为什么克己复礼就是仁？大致可以这样理解：克己是克服自私之心，多考虑别人的利益；复礼是按照礼的要求去做，也就是做正确的事；这样考虑和行动便是仁的表现。换句话说，只有仁人才能做到克己复礼。由此可见，仁和礼是同一事物的两面：仁为里，礼为表，仁为内容，礼为形式。

不仁的人自然是不考虑礼的；礼对他没有用处。所以孔子说：

> 人而不仁，如礼何？人而不仁，如乐何？（3.3）
> （人如果不仁，怎么来运用礼呀？人如果不仁，怎么来运用音乐呀？）

音乐的作用和礼相似，两者皆以和谐为目的。而只有仁人才希望有和谐。

智被认为是一种品德，因为它是对道的理解，而理解道是实行道的前提。

对孔子来说，关于自然界和生产的知识并不重要，重要的是为人和治国之道。所以他说：

> 君子谋道不谋食。……君子忧道不忧贫。（15.32）

他的学生樊迟问他如何种庄稼、种菜，他说他不如老农，接着说：

> 上好礼，则民莫敢不敬；上好义，则民莫敢不服；上好信，则民莫敢不用情。夫如是，则四方之民襁负其子而至矣。焉用稼？（13.4）

（在上位的人如讲礼，民众便不敢不尊敬；在上位的人如行为正确，民众便不敢不服从；在上位的人如讲信用，民众便不敢不以真实的态度对待。能如此，四方的民众就会背着孩子来投奔了。何必要学种庄稼？）

可见孔子希望他的学生理解礼、义、信等品德的意义，而不要忙于学习种地等一类具体的技术。

他的著名门徒之一子夏说的一句话，把智与仁密切联系起来：

博学而笃志，切问而近思，仁在其中矣。(19. 6)
（广泛地学习，坚守自己的志向，就切身的事多问，就眼前的事多思考，仁就在这里面了。）

为了修身和理解人生而博学，这样得来的智，自然会提高品德的修养。没有这种智的人，便像盲人一样，分不清是非，更谈不上治理国家了。又智又仁的人把国家治理好，民众就能安居乐业，农、工等业也就会兴旺发达起来。孔子批评樊迟要求学种庄稼，正是因为他没有理解这个道理；当然这也表示孔子对生产劳动的看法有偏差。

孔子对智者和仁者都有所赞美：

知者乐水，仁者乐山；知者动，仁者静；知者乐，仁者寿。(6. 23)
（智者爱好水，仁者爱好山；……）
知者不惑，仁者不忧，勇者不惧。(9. 29)

最后谈信。信包涵信用、忠实、诚恳等意思。没

有信这个品德,正常的人与人的关系和上下级的关系便不可能维持。孔子谈到信的时候说:

> 人而无信,不知其可也。大车无輗,小车无軏,其何以行之哉? (2. 22)
> (做人而不讲信用,那怎么行呢。大车没有輗,小车没有軏,怎么能行进呢?)

輗和軏是牛或马拉的车子上的关键的零件(把套牲口的横木与车辕子连接起来的木栓)。缺少輗或軏,就无法套牲口,车子也就走不了。人与人之间靠信联系;如彼此不诚恳,不讲信用,人际关系就谈不上了。

孔子在别的场合还说过"谨而信"(1. 6),"敬事而信"(1. 5)(谨慎地行事,讲求信实),"主忠信"(1. 8)(以忠信为主)等话。子夏也说:"与朋友交,言而有信。"(1. 7)前面引用过的曾参"吾日三省吾身"中的第二条是:"与朋友交而不信乎?"可见孔子及其主要弟子对信这个品德是十分重视的。

前面引的孔子对樊迟请学稼的评论中提到统治者应该坚持礼、义、信三条。有了这三条,就会取得民众的忠心和拥护。在和子贡的一次谈话中,孔子进一步强调信的重大意义:

> 子贡问政。子曰:"足食,足兵,民信之矣。"子贡曰:"必不得已而去,于斯三者何先?"曰:"去兵。"子贡曰:"必不得已而去,于斯二者何先?"曰:"去食。自古皆有死,民无信不立。"(12. 7)

（子贡问怎样治理国家。孔子说："使粮食充足，使武备充分，百姓自然信任上面。"子贡又问："倘若不得已，在这三者之中必须去掉一条，应先去掉哪一条呢？"孔子说："去掉武备。"子贡又问："倘若不得已，在剩下的两条之中必须去掉一条，应先去掉哪一条呢？"孔子说："去掉粮食。自古以来，人都不免死去。如人民对上面没有信心，是难以生存的。"）

孔子在这番话中把人民对政府的信任放在粮食的前面，意思是人民在他们信任的政府的领导下，终究可以克服暂时的困难，生产出足够的粮食；但是如果他们不信任政府，就会变得涣散、混乱，什么事都做不成，那就难以生存了。

Filial Piety and Respect for Brothers

A young man should be filial to his parents at home and respectful to his elder brothers out of doors. He should be cautious and trustworthy, love the multitude extensively and be close to those who are humane. If there is energy to spare, he can study the classics.(1.6)

What Confucius said here is important in that it indicates the stages of a young man's efforts at self-cultivation. First he should love his parents and brothers, then he should love the multitude, and after that, if possible, he should study the classics.

To begin by loving one's parents and brothers and then to go forward to love the multitude are steps towards one's acquisition of humanity. This perspective on life reflects Confucius' view on family life and family education. The family was very important in his eyes because generally people spent their early years with their parents and formed their characters under their influence. Thus the family influenced the direction of their lives. Besides, people's characters and behavior are revealed first in their families, because they have more contact with people in their families than with others.

We may call the family the cell of society. In feudal society based on agriculture, the position and function of the family are more important than in other societies, for each family is a unit of agricultural production. By laying emphasis on filial piety and respect for brothers, Confucius meant that all families should live in peace according to the norms and rites. This of course was of great help to the peace and stability of the whole society.

In Confucius' day and earlier, families — mainly noble families — were closely connected with political life. The feudal fief system made one noble family ruler of a particular area, and this power was hereditary. Within the family, a son or a younger brother should be filial or respectful to his father or elder brother; in political life, he should be loyal to his father or elder brother who was his leader. Thus filial piety merged into loyalty, and a filial son might at the same time be a loyal assistant. Such a relationship is clearly explained by You Zi, one of Confucius' disciples:

He who is filial to his parents and respectful to his elder brothers is rarely inclined to offend his superiors. He who is not inclined to offend his superiors is never inclined to

**rebel. The gentleman devotes his efforts to
the roots of things, for the Way grows from
them. Are filial piety and respect for brothers
not the root of humanity? (1.2)**

So in You Zi's view one who was filial and
respectful at home was not likely to offend his
superiors or cause trouble as an official. That is to
say, one's behavior as a son or a brother predicted
one's behavior as an official. Furthermore, he
considered filial piety and respect for brothers the
root of humanity. Every man should love his parents
and brothers, for they are the people closest to him.
If he does not, he is unlikely to have any love for
those who are not close to him.

According to Confucius, because a person's
parents have brought him up and loved him, he
should love them in return. A disciple named Zai
Wo said to his master that three years' mourning
for one's parents was too long, and that one year of
mourning would be enough. Upon hearing this, the
master asked him whether he would be at ease
eating good rice and wearing fine silk only one year
after his parents' death. The answer was in the
affirmative. Then the master said,

**If you are at ease, do so! The gentleman in
mourning finds no pleasure in eating good
food, no delight in hearing music, and no**

comfort in living at home. So he does not do these things. If you are at ease, do so!

After Zai Wo left, he continued,

How inhumane Yu (Zai Wo) is! A child is held in his parents' arms until he is three years old. The three-year mourning is observed everywhere. Does Yu have so little love for his parents that he cannot mourn them for three years after their death? (17.21)

He meant by this that showing filial piety to one's parents is something natural, an expression of true feelings, and a fitting return for the upbringing that one has received from them. This view may have been strengthened by Confucius' own experience in his early years, since his young widowed mother endured great hardships and difficulties while bringing him up and died when he was still young. All this, of course, he would never forget.

In keeping with Confucius' emphasis on family relations, *The Great Learning* put forward the theory of the four steps necessary for one to work for the people, namely: cultivating oneself, regulating the family, governing the state, and pacifying the whole country. These will be discussed in the following section.

孝 悌

> 弟子入则孝, 出则悌; 谨而信, 泛爱众, 而亲仁。
> 行有余力, 则以学文。(1. 6)
> (年轻人在家应孝顺父母, 出门应敬爱兄长; 应
> 谨慎而讲信用, 广泛地爱大众, 亲近有仁德的
> 人。做到这些之后还有余力, 就去学习古代文
> 献。)

孔子这一段话的重要性在于它说明年轻人修身的
几个步骤: 首先他应该爱他的父母和兄弟, 然后泛爱
大众, 做到这些之后再去学习经典。

从爱父母兄弟到泛爱大众, 可以说是向仁的目标
前进的途径。孔子的这个观点, 反映出他对家庭生活
和家庭教育的重视。人一般都在家庭里度过他的童年
和少年, 也在家庭里形成他的性格和品质。家庭对人
的一生的道路和作为有极大的影响。从另一方面看,
人的品质和行为也首先在家庭中表现出来, 因为人总
是生活在家庭中, 家里的人总是最为亲近、接触最多
的人。

家庭是社会的细胞。在以农业为主的封建社会
中, 家庭的地位及作用尤其重要, 因为小农生产是以
家庭为单位进行的。孔子强调孝悌, 也就是要求家庭

和睦，能够安居乐业，按常规生活，按礼办事。这当然有助于整个社会的和平稳定。

在孔子那个时代或更早，家庭——主要是贵族家庭——和政治的关系十分密切。分封制度使得一个贵族家庭成为一个地区的统治者，而且这种统治权是世袭的。从家庭关系上说，儿子应该孝顺父母，弟弟应该尊敬兄长；从政治关系上说，子与弟应该忠于作为上级的父与兄。这样，孝与忠便一致起来，孝子与忠臣可以是同一个人。这两者的联系在有子（孔子的一个著名的学生）的一段话中说得很清楚：

> 其为人也孝弟，而好犯上者鲜矣；不好犯上而好作乱者，未之有也。君子务本，本立而道生。孝弟也者，其为仁之本与！ (1.2)
> （孝顺父母，敬爱兄长的人，是很少喜欢触犯上级的；不喜欢触犯上级却喜欢造反捣乱的人是从来没有的。君子在根本处下功夫，根本建立起来了，道就会产生。孝顺父母和敬爱兄长该是仁的根本了！）

有子认为在家孝悌的人不会在外面犯上作乱。换言之，一个人的做儿子、做弟弟的行为就预示他以后做臣子的行为。他还进一步指出孝悌是仁的根本。人都应该爱自己的父母兄弟，因为他们是最亲近的人。如果连父母兄弟都不爱，就很难爱与自己不太亲近的人了。

在孔子看来，儿子应该爱父母是因为父母爱过他，把他养大。一次他的学生宰我对他说：父母死后，守孝三年，时间太长了，守孝一年也就可以了。孔子听后问他：父母死后一年便吃好米，穿缎衣，心里安不安？宰我说：安。孔子接着说：你要是心安，就这么办吧。君子守孝期间，吃好东西不觉得好吃，听音乐不觉得快乐，住在家里总觉得不安，所以才不做这些事。宰我出去以后，孔子又说：宰我真不仁呀！儿子生下三年，才离开父母的怀抱，所以守孝三年。宰我对已死的父母有三年的爱吗？（17. 21）

这也就是说，子女孝顺父母是很自然的事，是感情的流露，是对父母养育之恩的报答。孔子有这个看法，也许与他自己幼年及少年时期的经历有点关系。他的年轻的寡母，含辛茹苦，把他抚养大，在他刚成年的时候就死去了，这一切当然是他终身难忘的。

与孔子重视家庭及父子兄弟的关系相一致，《大学》一书中提出"修身、齐家、治国、平天下"的四步说，我们将在下一节中再做进一步的讨论。

Self-Cultivation

Confucius called one with a high moral character a *junzi* or gentleman and one without it a *xiaoren* or small man.

Originally *junzi* referred to a member of the ruling class and *xiaoren* to one under his rule. Confucius gave the two terms new meanings, distinguishing them on the basis of moral standards rather than social status. He said,

The gentleman knows what is right; the small man knows what is profitable. (4.16)

The gentleman reaches for what is high; the small man reaches for what is low. (14.23)

The gentleman often thinks of virtues; the small man often thinks of his native land. The gentleman often thinks of law; the small man often thinks of generous rewards. (4.11)

Confucius frequently made such comparisons in the hope that his students might understand that to be gentlemen they had to work hard at self-cultivation. This also involves habit and disposition, wherein a gentleman differs from a small man:

The gentleman sets demands on himself; the small man sets demands on others. (15.21)

The gentleman helps others to do good, never ill; the small man does the opposite. (12.16)

The gentleman is calm and not arrogant; the small man is arrogant and not calm. (13.26)

Sima Niu asked about the gentleman. Confucius said, "The gentleman is free from worries and fears." "Can a man be called a gentleman only because he is free from worries and fears?" Confucius said, "If a man finds nothing wrong when he examines himself, what is there for him to worry about or fear?" (12.4)

In short, a gentleman is humane, considerate towards others, entirely unselfish. It follows, naturally, that he is always calm and free from worries and fears.

Confucius further pointed out that a sound moral character is not something that one is born with, but something acquired through one's conscious effort at self-cultivation. He had a most important observation regarding this:

By nature men are pretty alike, but learning

and practice set them apart. (17.2)
"Learning and practice" here contains the idea of
aspiration and effort, which are most important. In
the section on humanity have been quoted two
sayings by Confucius which express a similar view:
"To practice humanity depends on oneself. Can it
depend on anyone else?" and "Is humanity far away?
It will come to me if I desire it."

The essential aspects of self-cultivation are
summed up in one saying by Confucius:

**Making no effort to cultivate virtue, to learn
and practice what has been learned, to follow
what is right, and to correct what is wrong
— these are my worries. (7.3)**

He meant that everyone should cultivate virtues;
for this purpose they should learn in earnest,
practice what they know is right, and correct what
faults they may have.

How learning can help one to cultivate virtues is
explained in the following dialogue in which
Confucius spoke with Zi Lu on six virtues and their
possible attendant faults:

**Confucius said, "You (Zi Lu), have you heard
about the six virtues and the six faults?"
"No," was the answer. "Sit down and I shall
tell you. He who loves humanity without
loving learning may be foolish; he who loves**

**cleverness without loving learning may be whimsical; he who loves trustworthiness without loving learning may hurt himself; he who loves straightforwardness without loving learning may hurt others; He who loves bravery without loving learning may cause trouble; he who loves resoluteness without loving learning may be arrogant."
(17.8)**

This tells us that a good virtue practiced blindly in a one-sided way is likely to produce a negative result and turn into a fault. Take humanity. If a man is bent on helping other people without investigating and analyzing the circumstances, he risks being deceived, and that is foolishness. A clever man loves to think, which is a good thing, but he may get unfounded and impractical ideas if he does not learn. A man who values only trustworthiness but cannot tell right from wrong may commit mistakes and harm himself. How the last three virtues may turn into faults is easy to understand, and it is also easy to find people with those virtues and faults. To prevent such deviations one has to learn and raise the ability to analyze and reason.

To follow what is right means to strive for correct thinking, speech, and action. This involves two dimensions. Firstly, one should exhibit pure thinking and high moral qualities in one's own conduct. For this Confucius praised his disciple Yan Hui:

> **Hui is a perfect man! No one else could bear his hardships — living in a poor hut with only a bowl of food and a gourd of water — but he is happy. Hui is a perfect man! (6.11)**

In dire poverty, Yan Hui was still happy, because there was nothing he felt regret for and he was at peace with himself.

Secondly, when conditions permit, a man of high moral qualities should work for other people's interests — help others to stand up and understand things. In talking with Zi Lu Confucius made this clear:

> **Zi Lu asked about the gentleman. Confucius said, "He cultivates himself so as to be earnest and reverent." "Does he stop there?" "He cultivates himself so as to bring peace and happiness to people around him." "Does he stop there?" "He cultivates himself so as to bring peace and happiness to the common people. In cultivating oneself to bring peace and happiness to the common people, even Yao and Shun may not have done enough." (14.42)**

That is to say, the ultimate purpose of one's self-cultivation is to bring peace and happiness to other people, first the people around one, such as parents, brothers, relatives and friends, and those one works with, and then all the common people. This thought is clearly explained in *The Great Learning*:

In ancient times those who wished to expound bright virtues to the whole country would first bring order to their states. Those who wished to bring order to their states would first regulate their families. Those who wished to regulate their families would first cultivate their own moral character.... When the moral character is cultivated, the family will be regulated; when the family is regulated, the state will be in order; when the state is in order, the whole country will be pacified.

Confucian scholars of later periods generally considered it their sacred duty to do these four things: cultivating their own moral character, regulating their families, bringing order to their states, and pacifying the whole country. To these objectives many would dedicate their whole lives.

How to deal with errors is an important part of one's self-cultivation. While no one is free from errors, some may admit and correct them, and others may cover up and gloss over them. Confucius encouraged people to redress their faults, saying:

A fault unmended is a fault indeed (15.30).

If you make a mistake, do not be afraid of correcting it. (1.8)

His disciple Zi Xia called one who tried to conceal his mistakes a "small man." (19.8) Zi Gong said something impressive on the same topic:

When a gentleman commits a mistake, it is like an eclipse of the sun or the moon: everyone sees it occur and everyone gazes up at its change. (19.21)

One who perseveres in doing all these things, whatever one's social status, is a humane man, a *junzi* or gentleman.

修 身

照孔子看来，有高尚道德的人是"君子"，没有高尚道德的是"小人"。

本来君子是指统治阶级的成员，而小人是指被统治的老百姓。孔子赋予这两个名词新的意思：按道德标准，而不是按社会地位，来区分这两类人。孔子说：

君子喻于义，小人喻于利。(4.16)

君子上达，小人下达。(14.23)

（君子向上通晓仁义，小人向下通晓财利。）

君子怀德，小人怀土；君子怀刑，小人怀惠。(4.11)

（君子多想到道德，小人多想到乡土；君子多想到法度，小人多想到恩惠。）

孔子多次做这样的比较，务使他的学生明确，只有加强道德修养才能成为君子。修养也涉及作风和性格。在这方面君子与小人也有明显的差别：

君子求诸己，小人求诸人。(15.21)

（君子严格要求自己，小人严格要求别人。）

君子成人之美，不成人之恶。小人反是。(12.16)

（君子帮助别人做好事，不帮助别人做坏事。*小

---

*另一种解释是君子帮助别人发扬优点，不帮助别人加重缺点。

人则反过来。)

君子泰而不骄，小人骄而不泰。(13.26)
(君子总是心地坦然而不骄傲，小人总是骄傲而
忧虑很多。)

司马牛问君子。子曰："君子不忧不惧。"曰："不
忧不惧，斯谓之君子已乎？"子曰："内省不疚，
夫何忧何惧？"(12.4)
(司马牛问怎样才是君子。孔子说："君子不忧愁
不惧怕。"司马牛说："不忧愁不惧怕就是君子了
吗？"孔子说："在内心反省时不觉得有愧，有
什么可忧愁可惧怕的呢？")

总之，君子是一个仁者，处处为别人着想，毫无
自私自利之心。从而他总是心地坦然，不忧不惧。

孔子还进一步指出，高尚的道德并不是生下来就
有的，而是努力修身的结果。关于这一点，他说了一
句十分重要的话：

性相近也，习相远也。(17.2)
(人的天性是相近的，但学习与实践使他们有分
别。)

这句话中的"习"字可以解释为习惯、学习、实
践等，总之是实际生活。这里面包括各人自己的愿望
和努力，而这是极为重要的。前面谈仁的一节里引过
孔子说的两句话就说明这一点："为仁由己而由人乎
哉？""仁远乎哉？我欲仁，斯仁至矣。"

孔子有一句话概括了修身的几个方面：

> 德之不修，学之不讲，闻义不能徙，不善不能改，是吾忧也。(7. 3)

他忧虑的四件事，如果从正面去说，就是修德、讲学、徙义、改过。人人都要培养自己的品德；为此就要认真学习，并实践所学到的道理；知道怎样做是正确的，就一定去做；如果有了缺点，就要改正。

关于学习与修德的关系，孔子在下一段话中讲得很清楚：

> 子曰："由也，女闻六言六蔽矣乎？"对曰："未也。""居，吾语女。好仁不好学，其蔽也愚；好知不好学，其蔽也荡；好信不好学，其蔽也贼；好直不好学，其蔽也绞；好勇不好学，其蔽也乱；好刚不好学，其蔽也狂。"(17. 8)

这是孔子和子路（仲由）的谈话。"六言六蔽"就是代表六种品德的六个字和可能伴随而来的六种蔽病，即愚蠢、流荡（无固定主张）、伤害自身、尖刻刺人、破坏捣乱，和狂妄自大。一种本来是好的品德，如果盲目地、片面地去履行，很可能走向反面，变成一种蔽病。拿仁来说，如果一个人只知道帮助人、做好事，对具体情况不做分析，那就有上当受骗的危险，反而成为愚蠢了。"好知"的人喜欢思考，这是好事，但如不学习，也会不着边际或脱离实际，得不到有根据的结论。只讲信用，不明事理，不知是非，会做错事，伤害自己。后三点是说直率可能刺伤别人，勇敢可能变成捣乱，刚强可能成为狂妄。为了防止这些偏差，必须加强学习，提高辨别是非的能力。

前面已经说过，义就是正确、合理。徒义就是使思想、言语、行动正确。一方面应该做到自己思想纯正，品德高尚。在这一点上，孔子很称赞他的门徒颜回：

> 贤哉，回也！一箪食，一瓢饮，在陋巷，人不堪其忧，回也不改其乐。贤哉，回也！ (6. 11)
> （颜回多么有修养啊！用竹篮子盛饭，用瓢喝水，住在破旧的房子中，别人都受不了这苦，颜回却始终是愉快的。颜回多么有修养啊！）

颜回尽管穷苦，但他心胸坦荡，无愧于人，所以始终是愉快的。

另一方面如果条件许可，有修养的人应该进一步为他人谋利益，也就是"立人"、"达人"。在和子路的一次谈话中，孔子指出这一点：

> 子路问君子。子曰："修己以敬。"曰："如斯而已乎？"曰："修己以安人。"曰："如斯而已乎？"曰："修己以安百姓。修己以安百姓，尧舜其犹病诸？" (14. 42)
> （子路问怎样才是君子。孔子说："修养自己，使自己诚恳知礼。"子路说："这就够了吗？"孔子说："修养自己，进而使周围的人安宁。"子路说："这就够了吗？"孔子说："修养自己，进而使百姓安宁。修养自己，进而使百姓安宁，就是尧、舜都没有完全做到呢。"）

这就是说，修养的目的是使别人得到安宁，先帮助自己周围的人，如父母、兄弟、朋友，以及一起工作的人，然后再争取帮助全体老百姓。这一思想在《大学》一书中得到进一步的说明：

> 古之欲明明德于天下者，先治其国，欲治其国者，先齐其家。欲齐其家者，先修其身。……身修而后家齐，家齐而后国治，国治而后天下平。

后世的儒家学者一般都认为修、齐、治、平是他们的神圣职责，终身奋斗的目标。

怎样对待过失（"不善"）是修身的一个重要方面。人都会犯错误，但有人能承认并改正错误，有人却掩盖和文饰错误。孔子鼓励人们改正错误，他说：

> 过而不改，是谓过矣。(15. 30)
>
> （有了过失不改，那就是真正的过失了。）
>
> 过，则勿惮改。(1. 8)
>
> （有了过失，不要怕改。）

他的门徒子夏把文饰过失的人称作"小人"(19. 8)。关于改过，子贡说了两句给人深刻印象的话：

> 君子之过也，如日月之食焉：过也，人皆见之；更也，人皆仰之。(19. 21)
>
> （君子的过失，好像日蚀和月蚀：犯错误的时候，大家都看见；改正的时候，大家都仰望着。）

能坚持做到以上说的几点的人，不论其社会地位如何，可以说是个仁人，或者是个君子了。

Chapter Five: On Government

In confucius' time, as has been mentioned, big states vied with one another to expand their territory, while small ones tried desperately to sustain what existence they could. In the midst of the incessant wars, the common people had a harder lot than ever. The rulers of states wanted to become richer and militarily stronger than their neighbors, and would stop at nothing in tricking and deceiving each other. Moral principles, if not entirely abandoned, played only an insignificant part in government and relations between states. At this time Confucius called on all rulers to rule by virtue and practice humane government. While it was obvious that his principles were inimical to their interests and could not be accepted, his political thought is of great significance and deserves careful study.

第五章 论政

　　前面已经提到，在孔子那个时代，大国竞相扩张，小国力求自保；战争不断，民不聊生；各国统治者致力于富国强兵，或以阴谋及策略取胜；道义原则，如果没有完全丢掉，也起不了什么大作用了。这时孔子向各国统治者提倡德治和仁政,显然不符合他们的要求，因而不会被采纳，但作为政治思想，却有其重大的意义，值得深入研究。

Rule by Virtue

Rulers of the Spring and Autumn Period generally resorted to harsh laws and severe punishments to make the people obedient. Confucius was opposed to this repression and upheld rule by virtue:

Guide them with government orders, regulate them with penalties, and the common people will try to avoid punishments, but will not have a sense of shame. Guide them with virtue, regulate them with the rites, and the common people will have a sense of shame, and abide by what is required of them. (2.3)

To Confucius government orders and penalties, and virtue and the rites were diametrically opposite ways of government. The former were coercive measures, which inevitably resulted in the common people trying hard to escape punishments while not feeling ashamed at evading orders. Virtue and the rites constituted for him a persuasive and educational approach, whose adoption would lead the common people to consider it a shame to disobey their leaders and try earnestly to meet all their demands.

In his view, guiding the common people with virtue presupposed that what was required of them was reasonable. Because of this they would be willing to carry out orders from the above. Regulating them with the rites implied that the rites were applicable to the common people. Here Confucius departed from the tradition that had come down from the Western Zhou: Rites should never apply to the common people, and punishments should never apply to the nobility.

The first prerequisite of rule by virtue is the sound moral character of the ruler himself; without this rule by virtue would be impossible. Confucius said,

An upright man will be obeyed even if no orders are given; a crooked man will not be obeyed even if orders are given. (13.6)

To Ji Kang Zi who had control over the Lu government Confucius said,

What need is there for killing in governing the state? The people will be good when you desire to be good. The virtue of the gentleman is like wind, and the virtue of the small man is like grass. The wind blowing over the grass will certainly bend it. (12.19)

So in Confucius' view, if the leader was upright and possessed correct thinking and behavior, the common people would work according to his wishes, and he would not have to give orders. Moreover, the people would try to think and behave in the right way. In other words, government is morality: "To govern means to be upright." (12.17)

Confucius compared the leader's thinking to the wind and the populace's to grass, which bends in whatever direction the wind blows. This comparison has at least two implications: the leader has a great influence, especially moral influence, on the populace; and the main responsibility for problems in government resides with the leader.

Under a sensible ruler, either an emperor or a local governor, the whole country or individual area tended to be peaceful and prosperous. But given a corrupt or immoral leader the situation became chaotic. Chinese history abounds in facts that serve to substantiate the above views.

The second prerequisite of rule by virtue is that one must put into important positions only virtuous and talented people.

Duke Ai asked, "What must I do to make the people believe in me?" Confucius answered, "Choose upright men and put them above the crooked, and the people will believe in you; choose crooked men and put them above the upright, and the people will not."

(2.19)

On other occasions Confucius talked about how good people could be discovered: mainly by studying public opinion. He said that a man disliked by many should be investigated, so should a man liked by many. (15.28) He further pointed out that an ideal man was one who was liked by good people and disliked by bad people. (13.24) The application of this standard would prevent dissemblers from getting government posts.

A virtuous ruler, when assisted by capable ministers, need not toil day and night to take care of all the affairs of state. In praising Shun Confucius said,

If any ruler carried out rule by nonaction, it was Shun. What did he do? He only sat reverently and solemnly, facing south in his place. (15.5)

According to legend, Yao chose as his successor Shun, who, assisted by Yu and Gaoyao, both selfless and capable ministers, reigned over an orderly and peaceful country, though he did not do much work himself. By praising Shun, Confucius perhaps meant to stress the force of a ruler's moral example and the importance of using virtuous men to govern.

What is interesting is Confucius' praise of rule by nonaction, which seems to be in agreement with

Taoist political thought. However, a careful study may reveal their essential difference. Confucian rule by nonaction is based on the moral excellence of the rulers — the king and his ministers. Under their influence and educated by them, the common people will know what is right or wrong, and will consider it a shame to do anything bad. Moreover, they will make an effort to abide by their leaders' requirement. This, as Confucius believed, should be the result of using virtue and the rites in governing a state. There would not be many issues and problems to preoccupy the rulers. The Taoists, on the other hand, deny the necessity of morality and social progress. To them primitive simplicity is the best way of life; government of any sort is therefore unnecessary*. These two views on nonaction have different bases and also predict different outcomes.

---

*See The Lao Zi, Chapter 80.

德 治

　　春秋时期的统治者一般都用严刑峻法来迫使老百姓服从自己的命令。孔子反对这种统治方法，主张德治：

> 道之以政，齐之以刑，民免而无耻。道之以德，齐之以礼，有耻且格。(2. 3)
> （用政令来领导民众，用刑罚来整顿他们，他们只求免于刑罚，而无羞耻之心。用道德来引导他们，用礼来整顿他们，他们就会有羞耻之心，而且达到上面的要求。）

　　孔子在这里把政、刑与德、礼作为两种对立的治国方法来提。政和刑是强迫手段，使用的结果必然是老百姓设法逃避刑罚，但并不觉得不切实服从命令是可耻的。德和礼则是感召和教育方式，采用这种方式会使民众从内心里认为不服从领导是可耻的，因而能自觉地实现领导的要求。

　　"道之以德"当然还包含要求于民的是合理的意思，这就更能使人民愿意服从领导。"齐之以礼"等于说礼也适用于民众，在这里孔子背离了西周以来所实行的"礼不下庶人，刑不上大夫"的原则。

　　德治的第一个条件是统治者必须是道德高尚的

人，否则德治无从谈起。孔子说：

> 其身正，不令而行；其身不正，虽令不从。(13.
> 6)

孔子对在鲁国执政的季康子说：

> 子为政，焉用杀？子欲善而民善矣。君子之德
> 风，小人之德草，草上之风必偃。(12. 19)

照孔子看来，领导者自身有德，思想行为正确，不下命令老百姓也会按照他的意图办事，也会努力使自己的思想行为正确。换言之，政治就是道德，"政者正也"(12. 17)。他把领导人的思想比作风，民众的思想比作草，风向哪边吹，草就向哪边倒。孔子这样说，至少表达了两点看法：一是领导者对民众有极大的影响力，尤其是道义上的影响力；二是政治上的问题，应由领导者负主要责任。

中国历史上许多事实证明上述的观点基本上是正确的。在有一个比较清醒的统治者（皇帝或地方官）的时候，很可能有一番太平景象。而当统治者是昏庸而荒淫的时候，必然是天下大乱。

德治的第二个条件是任用有德有才的人，即贤才。

> 哀公问曰："何为则民服？"孔子对曰："举直错
> 诸枉，则民服；举枉错诸直，则民不服。"(2. 19)
> （哀公问："怎样才能使民众心服？"孔子答道：
> "起用正直的人，把他们放在邪曲的人上面，民
> 众就服了。如果起用邪曲的人，放在正直的人上

面，民众便不服。")

在别的场合，孔子谈到怎样识别贤才：主要看大众的反映。他说：如果许多人厌恶一个人，那就要考察；如果许多人喜欢一个人，也要考察（15.28）。他还进一步说明，最好是好人都喜欢，而坏人都厌恶的人（13.24）。这样就可防止那种讨好所有人的好好先生被授予重任。

如果一个统治者，自己很有德行，又有贤才来辅佐他，那么他就不需要日夜操劳，亲自处理大小政事。孔子在赞扬舜的时候说：

> 无为而治者其舜也与？夫何为者？恭己正南面而已矣。（15.5）
>
> （能做到无为而治的大概只有舜吧？他做什么呢？自己恭恭敬敬，端正地坐在君王之位罢了。）

根据历史传说，尧禅位于舜，舜有贤臣禹和皋陶协助他治国，他无须做很多事情，天下也就大治。孔子称赞舜，大概是为了突出强调君王的道德榜样的作用和任用贤才的重要性。

有趣的是孔子也赞美无为而治，和道家的政治思想似乎不谋而合。但仔细研究，便可发现孔子和道家的主张有根本的差别。孔子的无为而治是以统治者（君王和辅臣）有高尚道德为前提的。在他们的感化和教育下，民众会分清是非，以做坏事为可耻，努力按照上面的要求去行事，即孔子说的"有耻且格"。这样当然就没有许多麻烦和问题需要统治者去解决。道家则否认道德的作用，反对社会进步，主张永远过原始性的简朴的生活，因而也就不需要有什么治理。*两者的前提不同，所指望的结果也是不同的。

*参看《老子》第八十章。

Humane Government

"Rule by virtue" stresses the moral qualities of the ruler and the measures he uses in governing his state, while humane government refers to the treatment of the populace. They are in fact the two aspects of the same thing. A humane ruler certainly carries out humane government. An inhumane one, on the other hand, inevitably resorts to despotic or tyrannical rule.

There is a story showing Confucius' hatred of tyranny:

While passing by Mount Tai, Confucius saw a woman crying sadly before a grave. He stood leaning against the horizontal bar of the coach and listened, and then asked Zi Lu to go over to her and say, "You are crying so sadly. Have you met with a great misfortune?" "Yes," she answered. "First my husband's father and then my husband was killed by a tiger. And now my son was killed too." "Why have you not left the place?" Confucius asked. "Because there is no tyrannical rule here" was the answer. At this

the master said to his students, "Remember that tyranny is fiercer than tigers."*

Confucius was opposed to tyrannical rule, but in his day the common people of almost all states suffered under it. So he did his utmost to persuade the rulers of the states to adopt humane government.

In some of his talks Confucius mentioned what humane government meant, for example:

Confucius was in the state of Wei, and Ran You was driving for him. Confucius said, "What a dense population!" Ran You said, "When the population is dense, what should be done then?" "Make them rich." "When they are rich, what should be done then?" "Educate them." (13.9)

This illustrates an important principle laid down by Confucius: the people should be made rich first and then educated. That is to say, it would be wrong to educate the people without making them rich, or to make them rich without giving them education. Neither way would bring about any good result. In contemporary expressions, to make people rich refers to the development of material civilization, while to educate them may be read as the

---

* See "Tangong" in *Records of the Rites*.

development of spiritual civilization. They have to occur simultaneously to ensure both the peace and stability of the state and the happiness of the people.

In light of Confucius' political thinking, the education given to the people should be that of the rites and music; in other words, moral education. To educate the people means to regulate them by means of the rites. As has been previously mentioned, the rites were moral codes, principles regulating human relations, and norm of conduct. It was believed that if the rites were universally observed, social order would be guaranteed, and, in turn, legal sanctions would be unnecessary. This view was to exert a great influence on Chinese society in later times.

In Confucius' time, rulers imposed two regular duties on the common people: taxes and corvee. Both were always too heavy for the people to bear and Confucius advocated reducing both as much as possible. He said, "Benefit the people where they can be benefited;... work those who can work at the right time;" (20.2) and "use the people at the right time." (1.5) In praising Zi Chan, an important minister of the state of Zheng, he said that Zi Chan was generous to the people and employed their services in a reasonable way. (5.16)

A significant point was made about taxation by

You Ruo, a disciple of the master's:

> **Duke Ai asked You Ruo, "We have had a lean year, and we do not have enough to meet our expenditure. What can be done?" You Ruo answered, "Perhaps you could take one-tenth of the people's income as tax." The duke said, "We are taking two-tenths of their income as tax, and still we do not have enough. How could the one-tenth tax rate be adopted?" You Ruo said, "If the common people have enough, with whom will you face insufficiency? If the common people do not have enough, with whom will you enjoy sufficiency?" (12.9)**

You Ruo was explaining very clearly, albeit indirectly, a truth: the wealth or poverty of a state is determined by the wealth or poverty of its people, who form the foundation and source of the wealth of the state. The primary concern of the ruler, therefore, ought to be to ensure they "have enough," and then he can try to resolve the problem of the state's expenditure. You Ruo was also expressing his teacher's belief regarding the enrichment of the people, while at the same time criticizing those rulers who extorted exorbitant taxes from the people.

In a talk with Zi Gong Confucius praised humane government highly:

Zi Gong asked, "What would you call a man who gives extensively to the common people and helps them to live well? Can he be called a humane man?" Confucius said, "Such a man is more than humane. He must be a sage! Even Yao and Shun would have found it difficult to do so!" (6.30)

After saying this, the master went on to explain the meaning of humanity as helping others to stand up when one wants to stand up oneself and helping others to understand things when one wants to understand things oneself. So humane government is the government guided by the spirit of humanity, an expansion and extension of the spirit. Just as humanity is the supreme virtue, humane government is the supreme principle for all rulers. After the Han dynasty many emperors and ministers declared their resolve to engage in humane government, and some of them may have made efforts in this direction and brought benefits to the people.

仁　政

　　德治是从统治者自身的品质和使用的治国方法而言，仁政则是从如何对待民众而言。两者实际上是同一事物的两个方面，是分不开的。统治者如是仁人，对民众必然实行仁政。反过来说，统治者如不是仁人，对民众必然实行暴政或苛政。

　　有一个故事说明孔子对苛政的痛恨：

　　　　孔子过泰山侧，有妇人哭于墓者而哀。夫子式而听之，使子路问之曰："子之哭也，壹似重有忧者。"而曰："然。昔者吾舅死于虎，吾夫又死焉，今吾子又死焉。"夫子曰："何为不去也？"曰："无苛政。"夫子曰："小子识之，苛政猛于虎也。"*

　　"式"就是靠在车前横木（轼）上表示敬意，"壹"是确实的意思，"舅"指丈夫的父亲。妇人告诉孔子虽然她家三代人死于虎，但还是不愿离开那个地方，因为那里没有苛政。孔子听后，就叫他的学生们记住，苛政比吃人的老虎还可怕。

　　孔子反对苛政，而在孔子那个时代，各国的老百姓几乎都遭受到苛政的迫害，所以孔子竭力劝说各国

------

* 《礼记》"檀弓"下。

诸侯实行仁政。

孔子在一些谈话中提到仁政的内容，如：

子适卫，冉有仆。子曰："庶矣哉！"冉有曰："既
庶矣，又何加焉？"曰："富之。"曰："既富矣，
又何加焉？"曰："教之。"（13.9）

（孔子到了卫国，冉有为他驾车。孔子说："人口
真多呀！"冉有说："人口已经很多，应该做什
么？"孔子说："使他们富起来。"冉有说："已
经富了，又该做什么？"孔子说："教育他们。"）

孔子在这里提出了一个很重要的原则：对人民应
先富后教。这也就是说，只是对人民进行教育而不设
法改善他们的生活，或者只是尽力使人民富裕而不进
行教育，都是不对的，都是不会有好结果的。用我们
今天的说法，富是物质文明，教是精神文明；必须两
个文明一起抓，才能使国家大治，人民幸福。

根据孔子的一贯思想看来，教育人民主要是进行
礼乐教育或道德教育，即"齐之以礼"。前面已经提
到，礼是道德的具体化，是处理人际关系的准则，是
行为的规范。如果人人遵守礼，社会秩序就有保证，
法律的制裁就不必要了。孔子的这个观点，对后世产
生了极大的影响。

当时统治者对民众的经常的要求有两大项，一为
赋税，一为劳役。赋税总是太重，劳役总是太多，因
而民众难以负担。孔子主张尽可能减轻民众的负担，
他说："因民之所利而利之……择可劳而劳之"；（20.

2)"使民以时"(1. 5)(在适当的时候使用民力);还在赞扬郑国大夫子产的时候说:"其养民也惠,其使民也义。"(5. 16)这里的"惠"就是恩惠,"义"就是合理。

关于赋税,孔子的弟子有若说了几句有意义的话:

> 哀公问于有若曰:"年饥,用不足,如之何?"有若对曰:"盍彻乎?"曰:"二,吾犹不足,如之何其彻也?"对曰:"百姓足,君孰与不足?百姓不足,君孰与足?"(12. 9)
> (鲁哀公问有若:"今年歉收,国用不足,怎么办呢?"有若答道:"何不征收十分之一的税呢?"哀公说:"我已征收十分之二的税,还不够,怎么能收十分之一的税呢?"有若说:"百姓富足了,君和谁一起感到不足?百姓不富足,君和谁一起感到富足?")

有若在这里虽然间接的,但是十分清楚地说明一个道理:国家的贫富决定于老百姓的贫富,他们是国家财力的基础和根源。因而统治者首先要设法使他们"足",然后才能解决国用问题。这和孔子说的"富之"的意思是一致的,也是对当时各国统治者的横征暴敛的批评。

孔子在和子贡的一次对话中高度赞颂仁政:

> 子贡曰:"如有博施于民而能济众,何如?可谓仁乎?"子曰:"何事于仁。必也圣乎。尧舜其

犹病诸。"(6. 30)

（子贡说："如有人广泛地给予人民利益，并能救济有困难的大众，怎么样呢？可以说是仁德了吗？"孔子说："这不仅是仁德，肯定是圣德了。就是尧、舜都会感到难以做到呢。"）

孔子在说了这几句话之后，解释仁的意思是"己欲立而立人，己欲达而达人"，可见仁政就是仁的精神在政治上的表现，是仁的精神的扩大。正如仁是最高的道德，仁政是政治的最高原则。汉代以后的许多帝王和辅臣都标榜行仁政，有的多少是朝这个方向努力，给人民带来一些好处。

Rectification of Names

Something Confucius once said about the rectification of names stimulated various interpretations and discussions by later scholars.

Zi Lu said, "The duke of Wei is waiting for you to take charge of the government. What will you do first?" Confucius said, "It may be necessary to start with the rectification of names." Zi Lu said, "You are so pedantic! How can names be rectified?" Confucius said, "You are being too rude, You (Zi Lu)! A gentleman should not talk about things he does not understand. If names are not correct, they cannot be used in a convincing way. If what is said is not convincing, things cannot be done successfully. If things cannot be done successfully, the rites and music cannot be spread. If the rites and music cannot be spread, punishments cannot be properly administered. If punishments cannot be properly administered, the common people will be at a loss as to what to do or where to go. So the gentleman

always gives things correct names which can be used in speech, and when he says something, he is certain that it can be carried out. The gentleman is never casual about anything he says." (13.3)

It is obvious that the term *names* as is used by Confucius here does not refer to the names of the concrete things of the world, but rather to concepts related to rites, music, punishments and people's behavior, or in other words, to ethical, ritual and political concepts. The "rectification of names" contains at least the following two meanings: everyone's social status and political position must be correct and properly founded; and everyone's behavior and speech must be in keeping with his status, position, and the requirements of the rites and ethical codes. Only when these conditions have been met, can his words be convincing and things done successfully. Otherwise, confusion and failure will certainly result.

At the time of Confucius' visit, the duke of Wei himself had a problem with this issue. He had been made Duke of Wei after his father, for some reason, fled to the state of Jin. Subsequently the father, escorted by Jin troops, wanted to return to Wei but was stopped on the border by his son's supporters assisted by troops sent by the state of Qi. It was a case of father and son becoming enemies and fighting for the power to rule a state. Confucius, to whom ethical codes and the rites were guiding principles, would naturally have disapproved of the duke's resisting his father's return. His talk with Zi Lu may have been connected with this controversy, but clearly he considered the rectification of names as a principle to be universally applicable, especially during a chaotic time like that of the Spring and Autumn Period. It was a time when incorrect names frequently cropped up as a result of people overstepping their authority or usurping high positions, and consequently they deserved to be denounced and rectified.

On other occasions Confucius made remarks indicating indirectly the necessity of correct names:

Confucius said of the nobleman Ji, "He has eight rows of dancers perform in the courtyard of his family temple. If this can be tolerated, what cannot be tolerated?" (3.1)

By using eight rows of dancers (sixty-four dancers in all) to perform in the courtyard of his family temple, the nobleman Ji of Lu committed a breach of the rites, according to which only the king could use so many dancers, a nobleman like Ji being entitled to four rows only. So Confucius proclaimed angrily that Ji would stop at nothing given that he had overstepped his authority to such a degree.

Do not be concerned with those government duties that do not belong to your post. (8.14) This means that if one interfered in the affairs of a department to which one does not belong, one would exceed one's authority — a case of incorrect names and unconvincing argument.

When the Way prevails in the country, the rites and music and punitive wars are decided by the king; when the country is in chaos, they are decided by princes and dukes. Princes and dukes can decide such things for no more than ten generations before they lose the power. Vassals lower than them can decide such things for no more than five generations before they lose the power. Their assistants can decide such things for no more than three generations before they lose the power. When the Way prevails in the country, power is not in the hands of vassals lower than princes and dukes. When the Way prevails in the country, the common people do not voice their opinions. (16.2) This is a comment on the abnormal political situation of the time caused by the Zhou king no longer having the authority he ought to have, and princes and dukes, like Duke Huan of Qi and Duke Wen of Jin, being powerful enough to decide the rites and music and wage punitive wars. But they could not enjoy such power for long, at most ten generations, for it ought not to be theirs. If vassals of lower station than princes and dukes, like the Ji family of Lu, usurped this power, they could not keep it more than five generations before they lost it. Their assistants could not keep this power, if they got it, more than three generations. This remark shows that Confucius wanted to maintain the king's authority and opposed the usurpation of power by princes and dukes, to say nothing of vassals of lower rank. It also shows that Confucius believed this abnormality, as it was incorrect in names and unconvincing, would arouse opposition, stir up criticisms by the common people, and could not last.

正 名

　　孔子关于正名说了一段话，引起后人很多解释和讨论。

　　　　子路曰："卫君待子而为政，子将奚先？"子曰："必也正名乎。"子路曰："有是哉，子之迂也。奚其正？"子曰："野哉，由也。君子于其所不知，盖阙如也。名不正则言不顺，言不顺则事不成，事不成则礼乐不兴，礼乐不兴则刑罚不中，刑罚不中则民无所错手足。故君子名之必可言也，言之必可行也。君子于其言，无所苟而已矣。"（13.3）

　　　　（子路说："卫国国君等待先生去主持政事，先生准备首先做什么？"孔子说："首先必定是正名了。"子路说："先生竟然这样迂阔。名怎么正呀？"孔子说："你太粗鲁了。君子对于自己不懂的事，就不要去谈了。如果名不正，话就说不顺。话说不顺，事情就做不成。事情做不成，礼乐制度就建立不起来。礼乐制度建立不起来，刑罚就不可能准确。刑罚不准确，民众就会手足无措，毫无办法。所以君子定一个名，必然是可以说得通的，而可以说得通的话必然是做得成的。君子对于说话是毫不随便的。"）

　　很明显，孔子在这里说的"名"并不是指一切事物的名称。这里的名和礼乐、刑罚、民众的行为有密切的关系，因而是涉及伦理、礼制和政治的名。"正名"至少有两层意思：每个人的身份和地位应该是合理的，有根据的；每个人的行为和言论应该符合他的身份、地位，符合礼制和伦理的要求。只有这样，话才说得顺，事情才办得成。否则就会导致混乱和失败。

当时的卫君就有名不正、言不顺的问题。卫君指卫出公辄，他的父亲蒯聩逃亡至晋国，卫国人立辄为君以后，晋国派兵把蒯聩送回，到了卫的边境，齐国又派兵协助卫国抵御晋兵。父子争位，变成仇人，引起战争。孔子从伦理和礼制出发，当然不赞成卫出公辄与父争君位。他与子路的谈话也许与此争端有关，但正名的原则有普遍的意义，尤其在春秋那样混乱的时代。那时僭越、篡位一类名不正言不顺的事件经常发生，都应该受到谴责和纠正。

孔子在别的场合还说了一些带有正名意思的话，如：

孔子谓季氏"八佾舞于庭，是可忍也，孰不可忍也？"(3.1)

鲁国的大夫季孙氏用八行共六十四人在庭院中表演舞蹈，违反了礼的规定（天子才可用八行，诸侯用六行，大夫应该只用四行）。孔子说这种僭越行为季氏都忍心去做，什么事他不忍心去做呀。

不在其位，不谋其政。(8.14)

不担任某一职务,就不应该干预与那职务有关的政事。如果干预,就是越权,就是名不正、言不顺。

天下有道,则礼乐征伐自天子出;天下无道,则礼乐征伐自诸侯出。自诸侯出,盖十世希不失矣;自大夫出,五世希不失矣;陪臣执国命,三世希不失矣。天下有道,则政不在大夫。天下有道,则庶人不议。(16. 2)

这是针对当时政治上的混乱状态而言的。周天子已经失去应有的权力,诸侯(如齐桓公、晋文公等)决定礼乐征伐等大事。这种僭越行为是不可能长久维持的,至多到十代。如果是比诸侯低一级的大夫如鲁国的季氏掌权,很少能维持到五代。若是大夫的家臣掌握国家大权,很少能维持到三代。孔子这一段话,表明他维护天子的权威,反对当时实际存在的诸侯甚至大夫掌权的现象,因为是名不正言不顺的,必然遭到反对,甚至被民众议论,是难以维持下去的。

Chapter Six: On Education

Confucius was China's first educator, and no doubt, therefore, one of the world's first educators. Before Confucius there had been a type of school education, but only for the nobles. Their children could learn to read, write, and study the classics at schools run by the government. Education, therefore, was one of their privileges; the common people had no right to it. During the Spring and Autumn Period, there were nobles who, after retiring from government posts, returned home and taught a few students from wealthy families in the neighborhood. This might be the earliest form of the private school. Confucius, however, was the first to set up a school for students from far and near and to develop significant educational principles and methodology of teaching.

Confucius was a teacher almost all his adult life. He began to teach when he was about 30 years old and continued until his death. History books tell us he had about 3,000 students, many of whom became renowned scholars and influential government officials.

One story testifies to his success in training capable people. When King Zhao of the state of Chu considered giving a fief to Confucius, his chief minister, Zi Xi, doubtful about the idea, asked the king, "Do you have any negotiator as good as Zi Gong? Do you have any adviser as good as Yan Hui? Do you have any commander as good as Zi Lu? Do you have any administrator as good as Zai Yu?" The king answred "No" to all these questions. Then Zi Xi warned him that assisted by such capable disciples, Confucius could be dangerous to Chu if he had a fief. Consequently, the king gave up the idea.*

*See "Biography of Confucius" in *Records of the Grand Historian*.

第六章 论教育

　　孔子是中国第一个教育家,无疑也是世界上最早的教育家之一。在孔子之前,学校教育是有的,但只有贵族才能享受。贵族子弟可以在官办的学校里认字读书,教育成了他们的一种特权,平民不能分享。在春秋时期,有些贵族成员不再从政,告老还乡之后,教几个家在附近的富家子弟,这便是私塾的起源。但孔子是第一个创办学校,广招学生,提出一系列重要的教育原则和教学方法的人。

　　孔子几乎毕生做教师。他从三十岁左右开始,直到去世,都在教学生。史书上说他有三千弟子,其中很多人成了有名声的学者或有影响的政府官员。

　　有一个故事证明孔子培养人才的成功。楚昭王考

虑授予孔子一块领地，他的令尹（相当丞相）子西颇
不以为然，问他："你有子贡那样好的使臣吗？你有
颜回那样好的辅臣吗？你有子路那样好的武将吗？你
有宰予样好的官员吗？"昭王对这几个问题都回答
"没有"。然后子西警告他说：孔子有这些能干的门徒
辅佐他，再得到一块领地，对楚国会构成一种危险。
昭王因此放弃了原来的想法。*

---

*见《史记》"孔子世家"。

Principles

The first important principle of education that
Confucius advocated was that all men were educable
and should indeed be educated. This may sound
commonplace today, but 2,500 years ago it required
great courage and wisdom for him to say anything
like it, since it was an open rebellion against the
tradition that education was for the nobles only.
Confucius brought education to the common people.
By doing this he made an immeasurable
contribution to the development of Chinese culture.
He said,

**I teach everyone without making
distinctions (15.39).**

An epoch-making declaration! And this was what
he did in practice. "I have never refused instruction
to anyone who presented me with ten pieces of dried
meat," he said. (7.7) A little dried meat was not an
expensive gift, so in effect he was asking for only
minimal tuition.

Confucius took teaching as his life's work and
never tired of it, partly because he believed in the
great potential of young people. He said,

The young are to be respected and feared. How do we know that future generations will not be as good as the present? (9.23)

His confidence in the young is an indication of his confidence in human and social progress.

Because of his fame as a scholar and teacher and the fact that it was easy to obtain his instruction, people from not only Lu but also other states came to study with him. Some of them were from wealthy or noble families, but many were from ordinary, even poor backgrounds. Yan Hui and Zeng Shen, for instance, were both poor men. Yan died in poverty at about forty, and Zeng often went three days without a meal and was unable to afford new clothes except every ten years.

Confucius' students varied to a remarkable extent in age. Zi Lu was only nine years younger than the master, while Zi Zhang, who was to become an important Confucian scholar, was 48 years his junior. Among his students were fathers and sons, such as Yan Lu and his son Yan Hui, and Zeng Dian and his son Zeng Shen.

To Confucius all men were educable because men were endowed with a similar nature. "By nature men are pretty alike," he said, "but learning and practice set them apart." (17.2) In his day this statement, which contradicted the prevailing view that the nobles were born superior to the common people, expressed the invaluable spirit of equality.

However, the door of Confucius' school was not open to women, against whom he was prejudiced. "Women and small men are difficult to deal with," he once remarked. "If they are close to you, they become impolite; if they are kept at a distance, they grumble." (17.25) He was not free from the influence of discrimination against women.

Confucius had a clear objective in educating his students: he expected them to be virtuous, to understand man and society, to have a good knowledge of the past and a clear vision of the future, and to devote themselves to the spreading and carrying out of the Way. He did not wish them to become experts in particular fields. He said, "The gentleman should not be an instrument," (2.12) — that is, an instrument used for a specific purpose. This view may have underlaid his criticism of Fan Chi when the latter asked to be taught how to grow crops and vegetables.

When he taught his students how to be virtuous men, he was also teaching them how to be government officials. To Confucius virtue and government are synonymous: "To govern is to be upright." (12.17) Rule by virtue and humane government, which he advocated, could be put into practice only by virtuous men. What Zi Xia, one of his well-known disciples, said might reflect his thinking in the respect:

An official with energy to spare should learn; a scholar with energy to spare should work as an official. (19.13)

The meaning of the former statement is quite clear: an official should acquire new knowledge to improve himself and his work. The latter statement was later often taken to mean that all scholars should try to become government officials. During the 1,500 years from the Sui to the Qing dynasty, countless scholars took the imperial examinations to enter the civil service. Zi Xia's view may have encouraged them to do so. In that period it was not a bad thing for scholars to work as officials, for they were generally more qualified for official posts than illiterate or poorly educated people. However, Zi Xia here is talking about a scholar "with energy to spare," which may imply that a scholar should first of all devote his time and energy to perfecting himself as a scholar, especially in the moral sense. Only then should he enter the government to carry out his ideals. This is in keeping with Confucius' idea of the gentleman cultivating himself to bring peace and happiness to all the common people.

For the purpose of training such scholars,

Confucius focused his teaching on the most important subjects. One entry in *The Analects* says,

Confucius taught four things: the classics, moral conduct, loyalty, and trustworthiness. (7.25)

The classics refer to those that had been compiled before Confucius and had been edited by him, namely, *The Book of Songs*, *The Book of History*, *The Book of Changes*, *The Book of Rites*, *The Book of Music*, and *The Spring and Autumn Annals*. They embody the wisdom of the ancient Chinese.

Moral Conduct was made one of the subjects because Confucius valued practice more than knowledge. He talked many times to his students about the relationship between knowledge and practice, expecting them to match their action to their words, put action before words, and be slow in talking and quick in doing things.

Loyalty and trustworthiness represent the moral qualities Confucius hoped that his students would acquire. As has been previously mentioned, loyalty is an aspect of humanity, while trustworthiness is the basis of inter-personal relations. Moreover, loyalty and trustworthiness are among the fundamental principles of government.

As we look at it today, the education Confucius developed may be called liberal or general education.

Science and technology were not taught and Confucius was opposed to his students studying them. His criticism of Fan Chi's request to learn farming illustrates this dislike. However, it would be wrong to conclude that his students were unable to do anything practical. On the contrary, among them were good commanders, men good at managing money matters, and coach drivers. Whether Confucius taught them these arts besides the classics and moral principles, however, is difficult to find out.

原　则

　　孔子的一个基本教育原则是：人人皆可教育，而且应该受到教育。今天这个主张听起来好像并不新奇，但在两千五百年前提出它确实需要极大的勇气和智慧，因为这是对当时的传统——只有贵族才能受教育——的公开反抗。孔子把教育带给普通百姓，从而对中国文化的发展做出了不可估量的贡献。他说：

　　　　有教无类。(15. 39)
　　　　（我教导所有的学生，不分类别。）

　　这是划时代的声明！事实上他也是这样做的："自行束脩以上，吾未尝无诲焉。"(7.7) 一个人只要送给他十条干肉（即束脩），就可以得到他的教诲。十条干肉是菲薄的见面礼，所以他要求的学费是极低的。

　　孔子终身为教师，诲人不倦，也可能是因为他对青年人抱有很大希望。他说：

　　　　后生可畏，焉知来者之不如今也？　(9. 23)
　　　　（年轻的人是令人害怕的，怎么能说以后的人不如现今的人呢？）

　　他相信青年也就是相信人类和社会总是会进步的。

由于孔子作为学者和导师的声誉远播,也由于拜他为师并不困难,所以不仅有鲁国,而且还有其他邦国的人都来求教。有的学生来自富家或贵族,更多的是一般人家,甚至是贫苦人家的子弟。例如已经提到过的颜回和曾参都是穷人。颜回在中年就贫病而死,曾参往往三天吃不上一顿饭,十年添不了一件新衣服。

他的学生在年龄上差别很大。例如子路只比老师小九岁,而子张,后来是一个重要的儒家学者,比老师小四十八岁。有父与子都来做学生的,如颜路和他的儿子颜回,曾点和他的儿子曾参。

孔子认为人人皆可教育,因为各人的天性是相似的。前面已经引过"性相近也,习相远也"这句话。在孔子那个时代,这句话与贵族生下来就比老百姓优越的传统观点相抵触,表现出宝贵的平等精神。

不过孔子的学校的大门对妇女是不开的。他对妇女有偏见。他说:"唯女子与小人为难养也,近之则不孙(逊),远之则怨。"(17. 25) 可见他没有能摆脱歧视妇女的影响。

孔子教育学生有一个明确的目标 要求学生成为有道德的人,了解人与社会,对过去有丰富的知识,对未来有明晰的构想,献身于道的传布和推行。他不希望学生成为某一行业的专家。他说:"君子不器。"(2. 12) 意思是君子不应该像一件器具那样只有一种用途。他批评樊迟想学种庄稼和蔬菜大概也是出自这种看法。

他教学生如何成为有道德的人,实际上也是教学生如何从政。对孔子来说,道德和政治是同义的:"政者正也。"(12. 17)孔子主张仁政和德治,当然只有道德高尚的人才能推行这种政治。他的著名门徒之一子夏说的一句话大概反映了他的思想:

仕而优则学,学而优则仕。(19. 13)
(从政者有余力应该学习,学习者有余力应该从政。)

前半句话的意思很清楚:从政的人应该学习新的知识来提高自己的水平和改进工作。后半句话一向被认为是鼓励学者做官。从隋朝到清朝的一千五百年中,不知有多少学者参加科举考试,走上宦途,这一思想一定起了促进的作用。在这个时期,学者做官并不是坏事;他们总比没有受过教育的人更有条件做好工作。但子夏说的是"学而优",也就是学有余力,意思可能是学者首先要努力提高自己,使自己在多方面,尤其在德行上,成为名副其实的学者,然后从政,以实现自己的理想。这和孔子说的君子"修己以安百姓"是一致的。

为了培养这样的人才,孔子有相应的教学重点。《论语》中有这样一条记载:

子以四教:文、行、忠、信。(7. 25)

"文"指在孔子以前就有的,并经孔子整理的典籍，即《诗》、《书》、《易》、《礼》、《乐》、《春秋》六部书。它们体现了古代中国人的智慧。

"行"即德行或社会实践。孔子一贯重视实践。他对学生多次谈到知与行，或理论与实践的关系，教导他们要言行一致，行在言先，讷于言而敏于行。

"忠"和"信"代表孔子希望学生培养的道德品质。如前述，忠是仁的一个方面，而信是人际关系的基础，同时忠和信也是执政的基本原则。

今天看来，孔子进行的教育可以说是文科教育或通才教育，科学技术是不教的。而且孔还反对学生去研究，他批评樊迟要学种地便是一例。但不能由此得出结论：孔子的学生不会做任何具体的事。相反，他的学生有的会打仗，有的会理财，有的会驾车。孔子除了教学生经典和德行，是否还教这些技能，已经无从查考了。

Methods

The Analects contains records of many conversations between the master and his students. Conversation, or question and answer, was probably the main method of instruction adopted by Confucius. Sometimes a student would come to him with a question, and he would give him a clear answer:

> **Zi Gong asked, "Why was Kong Wen Zi called 'Wen'?" Confucius said, "He was quick and loved learning, and was not ashamed of asking men below him for advice. That was the reason why he was called 'Wen'." (5.15)**

Kong Yu, a noble man of Wei, was given the posthumous title "*Wen*" (meaning culture or learning) after he died. Zi Gong asked why this title was given to him, and got an instructive explanation from the master.

Sometimes a student would express a view and the master comment on it:

> **Ran Qiu said, "It is not that I do not like your Way, but that I do not have enough strength." Confucius said, "He who does not**

have enough strength may stop to rest halfway, but now you set limits for yourself." (6.12)

Sometimes the master would start a conversation with a student to explain a theory to him, or direct his attention to a question, or point out the way forward for him. One example, which has been quoted in the section on self-cultivation, is his talk with Zi Lu about the six virtues and the six faults. Here is another example:

Confucius said to Zi Xia, "Be a scholar of the gentleman type; do not be a scholar of the small man type." (6.13)

At that time "scholar" referred to a status or a profession, denoting a learned man who was either a teacher or an official. Confucius, perhaps expecting that Zi Xia would become a teacher, advised him to exert himself to be a scholar with lofty ideals and a broad vision, one who put rightness before anything else.

Sometimes the master might talk with more than two students at the same time. On one occasion while he was together with Zi Lu, Zeng Xi, Ran You and Gongxi Hua, he asked each to speak about his wishes. (11.26)

A great number of entries in *The Analects* are the sayings of Confucius without the names of the listeners. These generally begin with "Confucius said," such as "Confucius said, 'The wise are free from puzzles; the humane are free from worries; the brave are free from fears;'" (9.29) and "Confucius said, 'Do not be concerned with those government duties that do not belong to your post.'" (8.14) They may have been uttered to many students, or to a particular student whose name was omitted when *The Analects* was being compiled.

Upon studying *The Analects*, the reader may be struck by two salient features of Confucius' sayings: the frequent references to real people and events, and the consideration of the needs of the listener.

Confucius mentioned or commented on many ancient personages such as Yao, Shun, Yu, King Tang, King Wen, King Wu, the Duke of Zhou, Baoyi, Shuqi, and many more personages of the Spring and Autumn Period, such as Guan Zhong, Zi Chan, Zhang Wenzhong, Liuxia Hui, Yan Pingzhong, Chief Minister Zi Wen, etc. Today we would term the citation of such references as the integration of theory and practice. To see how Confucius analyzed the merits and demerits of real people, we may as well examine his appraisal of Guan Zhong:

Zi Gong said, "Was Guan Zhong a humane man? Duke Huan killed Prince Jiu. Guan Zhong did not die for the prince, but became

the duke's chief minister." Confucius said, "Guan Zhong, as the duke's chief minister, helped him to become the leader of all the princes and dukes, and put the whole country on the correct road. To this day the common people are still benefiting from what he did. But for Guan Zhong, we might be wearing our hair long and loose and have our coats buttoned on the left. He did not need to observe petty faithfulness like a common man or woman and commit suicide in a ditch without being noticed by anyone." (14.17)

Guan Zhong was at first Prince Jiu's assistant. Both the prince and his brother, Prince Xiaobai, wanted to rule the state of Qi. In the struggle Prince Jiu was defeated and killed, while Prince Xiaobai won and became Duke Huan of Qi. Knowing that Guan Zhong was capable, the duke employed him as his chief minister. In appraising Guan Zhong, Confucius did not criticize him for not dying for the original master, but praised him for his contributions to the promotion of the position and culture of the whole country. This is a very good example of Confucius' way of analyzing problems: he grasped their essence and key points, without giving too much attention to petty things, whether they were right or wrong. It is easy to see what insight and help his students could get from a concrete analysis like this of people and events.

As a result of his good grasp of his students' strong and weak points, and their personalities and peculiarities, Confucius was able to give them the advice and guidance they needed. For this purpose, he would sometimes give different answers to different students who posed identical questions to him:

> **Zi Lu asked, "Should one take action as soon as one has heard a right thing?" Confucius said, "When one's father and elder brothers are living, how can one take action as soon as one has heard a right thing?" Ran You asked, "Should one take action as soon as one has heard a right thing?" Confucius said, "One should." Gongxi Hua said, "When You (Zi Lu) asked whether one should take action as soon as one has heard a right thing, you said that when one's father and elder brothers are living, one should not. When Qiu (Ran You) asked the same question, you said that one should. I am puzzled. May I ask about it?" Confucius said, "Qiu tends to hold back, so I tried to urge him forward; You has the courage of two men, so I tried**

to hold him back." (11.22)

Zi Lu and Ran You asked the same question, but Confucius gave them entirely different answers to help them overcome their relative weaknesses. Since these two disciples are mentioned several times in *The Analects*, it is possible for us to know something about their characters. Ran Qiu has been seen telling the master that he did not have enough strength to study and practice the Way, thereby revealing that he was not very bold or confident. On the other hand, Zi Lu once expressed his aspirations in this way: "If there was a state with a thousand chariots situated between more powerful states, and attacked by foreign armies and successive famines, I would govern it and could in three years make the people brave and morally sound." (11.26) He displayed self-confidence and an eagerness to achieve remarkable things.

Here is another example. Zi Gong, an eloquent negotiator, once asked the master, "What kind of man can be called a scholar?" The answer was:

He who has a sense of shame in his own conduct and can fulfill his mission when sent abroad by his prince may be called a scholar. (13.20)

When Zi Lu asked the same question, the answer was:

He who can help and learn from others and is genial may be called a scholar. He should help and learn from his friends and be genial to his brothers. (13.28)

It is easy to see that Confucius' answers matched the learning requirements of the two students. Zi Gong should be cautious about his missions abroad, and Zi Lu should be genial and ready to help and learn from his friends instead of being too forward and unyielding as he usually was.

In explaining his own teaching methods, Confucius said,

A student should not be taught unless he is anxious to understand what he does not understand, and should not be enlightened unless he is eager to express what he cannot express. When he is shown one corner of a square and cannot infer the other three corners, the teaching should not be repeated. (7.8)

The first sentence emphasizes the importance of the student's desire to learn or his motivation; the second emphasizes the necessity of reasoning and inference on the part of the student. A student with no desire to learn and unwilling to use his brains would render even a good teacher helpless. Confucius said,

I do not know what to do to one who never

asks "What am I to do? What am I to do?" (15.16)

Confucius encouraged his students to learn and think, and warned them not to learn without thinking or think without learning:

He who learns without thinking will be bewildered; he who thinks without learning will be in danger. (2.15)

Learning here may refer both to formal learning from books and informal learning from other people. Books and people provide one with all kinds of ideas and information, but they need to be sorted out, analyzed and digested before they can be of use to one. One must think while learning; otherwise one is sure to be bewildered. On the other hand, if one thinks all the time without learning from books or other people, one may think up strange ideas and even go astray, and that is dangerous. Confucius mentioned his own experience in this respect:

Once I spent a whole day thinking without eating any food and continued thinking for the whole night without sleeping, but it was useless. It would have been better to learn. (15.31)

Learning and thinking are like the two wings of a bird; only when a bird has both, can it fly.

方法

《论语》记载了孔子和他的学生之间的许多次谈话。谈话，或者是问答，也许是孔子所采用的主要教学方式。有时是一个学生向他提出一个问题，他给一个明确的回答，如：

> 子贡问曰："孔文子何以谓之'文'也？"子曰："敏而好学，不耻下问，是以谓之'文'也。"(5.15)

卫国的大夫孔圉死后谥为"文"，子贡问他为什么得到这个谥号。孔子说孔圉勤敏好学，又很谦虚，向水平或地位比他低的人提问题也不以为耻，所以得到"文"这个谥号。

有时一个学生向孔子说出一个看法，孔子予以评论，如：

> 冉求曰："非不说子之道，力不足也。"子曰："力不足者，中道而废，今女画。"(6.12)
> （冉求说："我不是不喜欢先生的道，但我的力量不足。"孔子说："力量不足，可以在半路上休息，而你是为自己划了界限。"）

有时孔子主动对一个学生讲一些道理，或要求他注意某一问题，或为他指出努力方向。前面引过的对

子路说的话（"由也，女闻六言六蔽矣乎？"……）便
是一例。再如：

> 子谓子夏曰："女为君子儒，无为小人儒。"（6.
> 13）

儒在当时是一种身份或职业，即从政或任教的有
学问的人。孔子可能预料到子夏以后会授徒讲学，因
而鼓励他做一个君子式的，不做一个小人式的学者。
也就是要站得高，看得远，以义为重。

孔子也有时和两三个或更多的学生同时交谈。例
如有一次子路、曾皙、冉有、公西华等四人和孔子在
一起，孔子要他们谈自己的志向（11. 26）。

《论语》中记录得最多的是没有提到对谁说的孔
子的话。这一类的话一般用"子曰"开头，如："子
曰：'知者不惑，仁者不忧，勇者不惧'"。（9. 29）又
如："子曰：'不在其位，不谋其政。'"（8. 14）这些
话可能是对很多人说的，也可能本来是对某一个人说
的，但转述的人在编《论语》时没有加以说明。

我们读《论语》会感觉到孔子的谈话有两个明显
的特点：一是常常联系真人真事，一是针对听话学生
的需要。

孔子提到并评论过相当多的古代人物，如尧、
舜、禹、汤、文、武、周公、伯夷、叔齐等；评论春
秋时期的人物就更多了，如管仲、子产、臧文仲、柳
下惠、晏平仲、令尹子文、陈文子、季文子、宁武子、

左丘明、孟之反、卫公子荆、史鱼、蘧伯玉、晋文公、齐桓公、卫灵公等。用我们今天的说法，这就是理论联系实际。且以对管仲的评价为例，来看孔子怎样具体分析一个人物的功过：

> 子贡曰："管仲非仁者与？桓公杀公子纠，不能死，又相之。"子曰："管仲相桓公，霸诸侯，一匡天下，民到于今受其赐。微管仲，吾其被发左衽矣。岂若匹夫匹妇之为谅也，自经于沟渎而莫之知也？"（14．17）

> （子贡说"管仲不是一个仁者吧？齐桓公杀了公子纠，管仲不能为公子纠而死，还做了桓公的宰相。"孔子说："管仲做桓公的宰相，使桓公成了诸侯的领袖，使各国走上正确道路，人民到今天还得到他的好处。要不是因为有管仲，我们恐怕都披着头发，衣襟开在左边了。他岂能像普通人一样，遵守小节，在山沟中自杀，还没有人知道呢。"）

管仲本来是辅佐齐国的公子纠的。公子纠和他的哥哥公子小白争夺齐国的统治权，失败被杀。小白成了齐桓公，因管仲有才，用他为相。孔子评价管仲，并不因为他没有为原来的主子公子纠而死便批评他，而是赞扬他对整个中国的地位和文化所做的贡献。因为当时的中国受到北方异族的危胁，如果没有管仲的领导，中原各诸侯国很可能被人征服，遵从了异族披发左衽的风俗。这是一个很生动的例子，说明孔子从大处着眼看问题，而不过多地注意小节。这样具体地分析人和事，对学生的启发和帮助是可想而知的。

孔子很了解他的学生的长处和短处，性格和特点，因而能给予他们最有帮助的教导。为了这个目的，他有时就同一个问题对不同的学生做出不同的回答。

> 子路问："闻斯行诸？"子曰："有父兄在，如之何其闻斯行之？"冉有问："闻斯行诸？"子曰："闻斯行之。"公西华曰："由也问闻斯行诸，子曰：'有父兄在'；求也问闻斯行诸，子曰：'闻斯行之'。赤也惑，敢问。"子曰："求也退，故进之；由也兼人，故退之。"（11.22）
>
> （子路问："听到正确的话是不是就要做？"孔子说："还有父亲、哥哥在，怎么能听到了就做呢？"冉有问："听到正确的话是不是就做？"孔子说："听到了就该做。"公西华说："仲由问听到了是否就要做，先生说有父亲、哥哥在；冉求问听到了是否就该做，先生说听到了就该做。我不清楚，想问一下。"孔子说："冉求做事往往退缩，所以我要他向前迈；仲由却想一个人做两个人的事，所以我要他往后退。"）

子路和冉求问了相同的问题，孔子做了相反的答复，目的是帮助他们克服各自的弱点。《论语》提到这两个人好几次，从中我们可以多少知道一点他们的性格。前面引的冉求说"力不足也"，表明他缺少勇气和信心。子路在谈自己的志向时说:"千乘之国,摄乎大国之间,加之以师旅,因之以饥馑;由也为之,比及三年,可使有勇,且知方也。"(11.26)(有一千辆兵车的国家,夹在大国中间,外有军事压迫,内有灾荒,让我去治理,只要三年,可使民众有勇气,而且懂得道义。)可见他对自己很有信心,而且很想做一番事业。

再举一例。子贡有口才,是谈判能手。一次他问先生"何如斯可谓之士矣?"先生说:

> 行己有耻,使于四方,不辱君命,可谓士矣。
> (13.20)
> (在行为上能知耻,出使外国,能很好地完成君主给的使命,就可以称为士了。)

子路也问了同样的问题,先生的答复是:

> 切切偲偲,怡怡如也,可谓士矣。朋友切切偲偲,兄弟怡怡。(13.28)
> (能够互相切磋,又能和悦相处,就可以称为士了。朋友之间互相切磋,兄弟之间和悦相处。)

这两次答复的针对性是很明显的:子贡应该谨慎对待出使四方的任务;子路则应该更为和悦,更易于和朋友切磋,而不应过分地直率刚强。

孔子自己谈他的教学方法时说:

> 不愤不启,不悱不发。举一隅不以三隅反,则不复也。(7.8)
> (学生如不求理解就不启发他,如不想表达就不

开导他。给他看一个角，还不能推想其他三个角，就不重复教他。)

前面两点强调学生的学习愿望或主动性，最后一点强调动脑筋思考及推想的重要性。对于没有学习愿望、不肯动脑筋的人，再好的老师也没有办法。孔子说：

不曰："如之何，如之何"者，吾末如之何也已矣。(15.16)

(对一个从不说"怎么办、怎么办"的人，我也不知道怎么办了。)

孔子鼓励学生把学习与思考结合起来，不要只学习而不思考，也不要只思考而不学习：

学而不思则罔，思而不学则殆。(2.15)

"罔"是迷惘的意思，"殆"是危险的意思。这里的"学"可以指向书本学习，也可以指向别人学习。从书本和人们那里可以得到各种各样的观点和材料，但为了使它们变得有用，还得加以整理、分析、消化，这就是思考，否则就会迷惘。在另一方面，如果只是思考而不向书本或别人学习，那就很可能想入非非，甚至走上危险的道路。孔子还提到他自己的经验：

吾尝终日不食，终夜不寝，以思，无益，不如学也。(15.31)

也许可以把学与思比作鸟的双翼。鸟必须有双翼，才能飞翔。

Teacher-Student Relationship

At this earliest school in China, there was a unique teacher-student relationship. Confucius and his students were united on the basis of the Way which the master formulated. They worked for the same objective and cause — the propagation and realization of the Way. For this reason, Confucius showed deep concern for and loved his students, always ready to answer their questions, and gave them instruction and criticism. His students, in return, were unreservedly loyal and reverent towards him; some of them accompanied him on his journey through the states, sharing with him all the attendant difficulties and dangers. He related to them not only as teacher to student, but also as father to son, and as friend to friend and comrade to comrade.

The following are a few dialogues from *The Analects* and a story from the biography of Confucius in *Records of the Grand Historian* which illustrate some facets of the moving relationship between the master and his students.

When Yan Yuan (Yan Hui) and Ji Lu (Zi Lu)

were standing beside him, Confucius said, "Why not let me hear what each of you wishes to do?" Zi Lu said, "I wish to share my carriage and horses, clothes and furs, with my friends, and will have no regrets if they are damaged." Yan Yuan said, "I wish to have merits and not to boast of them, and have achievements and not to show them." Zi Lu said, "May we hear what you wish to do?" Confucius said, "I wish to make old people live in peace, friends trust me, and youngsters remember me." (5.26)

The spirit of equality with which Confucius treated his students can be seen in this short dialogue. He asked them to talk about their wishes, and they also asked him to talk about his. He did not put on airs or hesitate, but told them in all sincerity what he wished to do.

Confucius went to Wucheng, where he heard the sound of stringed instruments and singing. Smiling, he said, "To kill a chicken one does not have to use an ox-knife." Zi You said in answer, "Some time ago I heard you say, 'A gentleman who has learned the Way loves other men, and a small man who has learned the Way is easy to use.'" Confucius said, "My friends, Yan (Zi You) is

correct. Just now I said that in fun." (17.4)

At that time Yan Yan (Zi You), one of the master's students, was the magistrate of Wucheng. Confucius went there and heard music and songs. He knew that Yan Yan was giving the people education in the rites and music. By saying "To kill a chicken one does not have to use an ox-knife" he meant that in order to govern a small place like Wucheng, the rites and music, which contained profound truths, might not be necessary. After hearing Yan Yan repeating what he had said in the past, Confucius said at once to those accompanying him that Yan was correct and that a moment before he had meant to make fun of the young magistrate. This little incident shows that Confucius did not think that everything he said expressed a truth which his students had to accept unquestioningly. This democratic spirit was, and still is, valuable in the academic field.

In fact, Confucius hoped that his students would have views that differed from his. Once he said, "Hui is not someone who gives me help. He is never displeased with what I say." (11.4) For Yan Hui he usually had nothing but praise. The above remark seems to be the only one in which he sounded critical of him.

Once he praised Yan Hui in this way:

Confucius said to Zi Gong, "Who is better, you or Hui?" The answer was, "How dare I compare with Hui? When he is told one thing, he knows ten; when I am told one thing, I know only two." Confucius said, "You cannot compare with him. Neither you nor I can compare with him." (5.9)

The original of the last sentence may also be construed as meaning "I agree that you cannot compare with him." But it should not be surprising that Confucius said he could not compare with Yan Hui, since he always considered modesty an important virtue.

To a student who had done something wrong, Confucius would give severe criticism, for instance:

The Ji family was richer than the Duke of Zhou, but still Qiu was raking in money to add to their wealth. Confucius said, "He is no disciple of mine. You who are my students may beat the drum and attack him." (11.17)

Ji refers to Ji Kang Zi, a noble man of Lu. He was richer than the Duke of Zhou (descendant of the Duke of Zhou who helped to found the dynasty), but Ran Qiu, while working for him, helped to amass money from the people. Confucius was angry at this and called on other students to denounce him.

Confucius would continue instructing his students under extremely difficult conditions. How he did this is described in the following story from the biography of Confucius in *Records of the Grand Historian*.

During his travels through the states, Confucius was once surrounded by hostile men between Chen and Cai. Cut off from supplies he and his followers were so hungry and exhausted that they could hardly move.

Well aware that the disciples were unhappy, Confucius called in Zi Lu and asked, "*The Book of Songs* says, 'Though not a buffalo or a tiger, I am wandering in the wilderness.' Is my Way wrong? Why am I in this plight?"

Zi Lu said, "Is it because we are not humane that others do not believe in us? Is it because we are not wise that others will not let us pass?"

Confucius said, "Is that so? If all humane men had been believed in, Boyi and Shuqi* would not have died. If all wise men had been

---

*Boyi and Shuqi were princes of a state in the Shang dynasty. After Zhou conquered Shang, they would rather die of hunger than eat Zhou food. Prince Bigan was the uncle of the last king of the Shang. He repeatedly warned the king against doing evil things, and the king killed him.

allowed to pass, Prince Bigan* would not have been killed."

Zi Lu left and Zi Gong came in. Confucius said, "*The Book of Songs* says, 'Though not a buffalo or a tiger, I am wandering in the wilderness.' Is my Way wrong? Why am I in this plight?"

Zi Gong said, "Your Way is too great and lofty to be accepted by the world. Could you lower it a little?"

Confucius said, "A good farmer can sow seeds but cannot always harvest. A good craftsman can do clever work but cannot always please his customers. A gentleman can cultivate his Way, lay down principles and put them into a system, but cannot always be accepted. Now you are not cultivating your Way but seeking to be accepted. You are not aiming high."

Zi Gong left and Yan Hui came in. Confucius said, "*The Book of Songs* says, 'Though not a buffalo or a tiger, I am wandering in the wilderness.' Is my Way wrong? Why am I in this plight?"

Yan Hui said, "Your Way is too lofty to be accepted by the world. However, so long as you pursue it, it is not your fault that it is

not accepted. That just shows you are a gentleman! It would be our shame if our Way had not been cultivated. Now that it is fully cultivated but is not followed, it is the shame of the rulers of the states. It is not your fault that it is not accepted. That just shows you are a gentleman!"

Confucius happily smiled, saying, "Well said, Yan's son! I would be glad to take care of your wealth if you were rich!"

This account reveals Confucius' elevated thinking and steadfast personality. Despite being in great difficulty and danger, he would not for a moment consider lowering or changing his principles merely in order to be understood by those opposed to him. He was prepared to follow the principle that a humane man never gives up humanity to save his life but sacrifices his own life to realize humanity.

The story also tells us that Confucius would link his moral and ideological instructions with the contemporary issues facing his students. Zi Lu and Zi Gong had doubts about the practicability of their master's Way, so Confucius analyzed their views and pointed out where they were in error. Yan Hui said something correct, and he expressed his approval at once.

Moreover, we see in the story how the teacher

and his students related to each other. The students would tell the teacher frankly what was on their minds, and if they were wrong, the teacher would give them straightforward criticisms. They understood and loved each other, and were sincere and close to each other, just like members of a family.

There are many instances when the students' loyalty to and love for their teacher are displayed. One entry in *The Analects* says:

When Confucius was detained in Kuang, Yan Hui was the last to join him. Confucius said, "I thought you had died." Yan Hui said, "As you are alive, how dare I die?" (11.23)

Another entry in the book records how Zi Gong compared himself with his teacher:

Shusun Wushu said to other nobles at court, "Zi Gong has more merits than Zhongni (Confucius)." Zifu Jingbo told Zi Gong about it. Zi Gong said, "It is like the wall enclosing a house. My wall only reaches the shoulder, and one can see over its splendid rooms. The master's wall is very high; one who cannot enter its gate cannot see the grand ancestral temple and magnificent halls and rooms. And very few can find its gate. Therefore such a comment is quite natural."

(19.23)

Yan Hui's and Zi Gong's words are very moving. One expressed with heartfelt emotion that he would always follow his teacher, to the point of living and dying with him; the other explained with deep sincerity and conviction his own mediocrity and his teacher's greatness. It was only natural that this teacher-student relationship should be taken as a model in later ages, since it promoted such strong bonds between teacher and student, encouraged mutual respect, and fostered love of learning and dedication to the Way.

In every sense, Confucius was a great teacher.

师生关系

在这个中国最早的学校里，师生关系也有特色。孔子和他的弟子是在孔子倡导的道的基础上结合在一起的。他们有一个共同的目标和事业——道的传布和推行。因此，孔子对他的学生十分关心爱护，随时解答他们的问题，给他们教导或批评。而学生对老师则无限爱戴和忠诚，有的陪同他访问各国，度过艰难的、有时是危险的年月。孔子与学生，不仅是师生，而且也是父子，朋友和同志。

下面我们从《论语》中引几段话，还从《史记》"孔子世家"一章中引一段故事，来从几个侧面说明孔子和他的学生的感人的关系。

颜渊、季路侍。子曰："盍各言尔志。"子路曰："愿车马、衣轻裘，与朋友共敝之而无憾。"颜渊曰："愿无伐善，无施劳。"子路曰："愿闻子之志。"子曰："老者安之，朋友信之，少者怀之。"（5.26）

（颜渊和季路站在孔子身边。孔子说："何不说说你们的志向？"子路说："愿意与朋友共同使用我的车马衣服，用坏了也不觉得遗憾。"颜渊说："愿意自己有长处，但不夸耀它；对人有功劳，但不表白它。"子路说："也想听听您的志愿。"孔

子说:"使老年人安定,朋友信任,年轻人怀念
我。")

从这个简短的对话中,可以看到孔子以平等的精
神对待他的学生。他要学生谈谈自己的志向,学生说
希望听到他的志向,他并不摆架子,也不推诿,而是
认真地谈出自己的想法。

子之武城,闻弦歌之声。夫子莞尔而笑,曰:"割
鸡焉用牛刀?"子游对曰:"昔者偃也闻诸夫子
曰:'君子学道则爱人,小人学道则易使也。'"子
曰:"二三子,偃之言是也。前言戏之耳。"(17.
4)

(孔子到了武城,听到弹琴唱歌的声音。孔子微
笑,说:"割鸡哪里用得着宰牛的刀?"子游答
道:"以前我听老师说过:'君子学道就会爱人,
小人学道就容易听指挥。'"孔子说:"你们听见
了,言偃的话是对的。我刚才说的话不过是和他
开玩笑罢了。")

当时孔子的学生言偃(即子游)为武城宰(相当
县长)。孔子去玩,听到弦歌之声,知道言偃对百姓
进行礼乐教育。他说"割鸡焉用牛刀",意思是治理
这个小地方,何必用礼乐的大道。在听到言偃重复他
过去说过的话后,他立刻对同游的人说明言偃的话是
对的,刚才不过是和这个年轻的县长开个玩笑。这个
小插曲表明孔子并不认为自己的每句话都是真理,学
生只能接受而不能怀疑或讨论。在学术问题上,这样

的民主精神过去和现在都是难能可贵的。

事实上孔子希望学生对他的观点提出不同的看法。他说:"回也非助我者也,于吾言无所不说。"(11.4)(颜回不是能帮助我的人,他对我说的话没有不感到喜悦的。)孔子对颜回一向是称赞的,大概只有这一句话有点批评的意味。

在称赞颜回时,有这样一次:

子谓子贡曰:"女与回也孰愈?"对曰:"赐也何敢望回?回也闻一以知十,赐也闻一以知二。"子曰:"弗如也。吾与女弗如也。"(5.9)

(孔子对子贡说:"你和颜回哪个强些?"子贡答道:"我怎么能和颜回比?他听到一点,就可以知道十点;我听到一点才能知道两点。"孔子说:"你是不如他。我与你都不如他。")

最后一句话中的"与"字有两个可能的解释:一是相当于"和"字,一是同意的意思。就孔子重视谦逊的美德来看,他说自己不如颜回也是很自然的。

但孔子对做了错事的学生也会严厉地批评,例如:

季氏富于周公,而求也为之聚敛而附益之。子曰:"非吾徒也,小子鸣鼓而攻之可也。"(11.17)

(季氏比周公更富,冉求还为他多方搜刮,增加他的财富。孔子说:"冉求不是我的门徒。你们可以打起鼓去攻击他。")

季氏(季康子)是鲁国的贵族,本来比王朝的周公（周朝初期的周公的后代）还要富，但冉求在为他服务时还帮他搜刮民财，因此孔子很生气，号召其他的学生去攻击他。

现在看《史记》"孔子世家"中的一段，它描写孔子怎样在极为艰难困苦的条件下对学生进行教育。当时孔子在陈、蔡之间，被反对者包围，断了粮食，随从的人又病倒了，情况很危急。

孔子知弟子有愠心，乃召子路而问曰："诗云'匪兕匪虎，率彼旷野'。吾道非邪？吾何为于此？"子路曰："意者吾未仁邪？人之不我信也。意者吾未知邪？人之不我行也。"孔子曰："有是乎！由，譬使仁者而必信，安有伯夷、叔齐？使知者而必行，安有王子比干？"

子路出，子贡入见。孔子曰："赐，诗云'匪兕匪虎，率彼旷野'。吾道非邪？吾何为于此？"子贡曰："夫子之道至大也，故天下莫能容夫子。夫子盖少贬焉？"孔子曰："赐，良农能稼而不能为穑，良工能巧而不能为顺。君子能修其道，纲而纪之，统而理之，而不能为容。今尔不修尔道而求为容。赐，而志不远矣。"

子贡出，颜回入见。孔子曰："回，诗云'匪兕匪虎，率彼旷野'。吾道非邪？吾何为于此？"颜回曰："夫子之道至大，故天下莫能容。虽然，夫子推而行之，不容何病？不容然后见君子。夫道之不修也，是吾丑也。夫道既已大修而不用，是有国者之丑也。不容何病，不容然后见君子。"

孔子欣然而笑曰:"有是哉颜氏之子! 使尔多财,吾为尔宰。"

这段叙述显示出孔子的崇高思想和伟大人格。当时他的处境极为困难和危险,但他根本不考虑改变或降低自己的主张,以求得反对他的人的谅解。他随时准备实行他所说的"无求生以害仁,有杀身以成仁"的原则。

这个故事也告诉我们孔子善于结合实际,对学生进行生动的思想教育。子路和子贡对老师的道是否能被人接受有所怀疑,孔子分析他们的看法,指出他们的错误所在。颜回发表了正确的意见,孔子立刻加以肯定。

这段描写还告诉我们孔子和他的学生有什么样的关系。学生能坦率地把自己的想法告诉老师,老师能直截了当地指出学生的错误。由此也可以看出他们互相了解,互相爱护,诚恳相待,亲密无间,像父子或兄弟一样。

关于学生对老师的忠诚和爱戴例子也很多。《论语》中有这样一段话:

子畏于匡,颜渊后。子曰:"吾以女为死矣。"曰:"子在,回何敢死?"(11. 23)

(孔子在匡被包围,颜渊落在后面。孔子[见到他时]说:"我以为你死了。"颜渊说:"先生还在,我怎么敢死呢?")

还有一段子贡比较孔子和他自己的话:

　　叔孙武叔语大夫于朝曰:"子贡贤于仲尼。"子服
景伯以告子贡。子贡曰:"譬之宫墙,赐之墙也
及肩,窥见室家之好。夫子之墙数仞,不得其门
而入,不见宗庙之美,百官之富。得其门者或寡
矣。夫子之云,不亦宜乎。"(19.23)
　　(叔孙武叔在朝廷中对大夫们说"子贡比孔子更
有德才。"子服景伯把这句话告诉了子贡。子贡
说:"拿围墙作比喻来说吧。我的围墙只有肩膀
高,在墙外可以看到里面房屋的好处。孔子的围
墙有几丈高,如果进不了大门,就看不见里面的
宗庙的美好,房屋的富丽。但能找到大门的人或
许很少。叔孙先生那么说,也就有道理了。")

　　颜回和子贡的话多么感人!一个用肺腑之言表示
他要永远追随老师,生死与共;一个以极大的诚恳和
信念说明自己的平庸和老师的伟大。这样的师生关系
被后世当作楷模是很自然的事情,因为这种关系促进
了师生之间的感情与互敬,加强了对学问的热爱和对
道的奉献精神。

　　不论从哪个意义上说,孔子都是一个伟大的教
师。

Chapter Seven: On the Will of Heaven, the Mean and Other Subjects

Morality, the rites, government, and education were the questions Confucius discussed most often with his students, and they were probably the questions with which he was mainly concerned. It appears that he considered them the burning issues of the day. However, he also gave thought to fundamental laws of the universe, relations between Heaven and man, ways of thinking, and other subjects. He did not say much about, but nevertheless expressed important views on, these questions.

第七章 论天命、中庸及其他

　　孔子与学生讨论的最多的,可能也是他思考的最多的问题,是德、礼、政及教育等。显然他认为这些是亟待解决的,因而给予它们极大的注意。但是他也研究宇宙的基本规律、天人关系、思想方法等问题,在这些方面虽然谈得不多,但也发表了重要的见解。

The Will of Heaven

It was only natural that more than 2,000 years ago people should have believed that Heaven or God decided and controlled everyone and everything. At that time men did not have enough scientific knowledge with which to explain such strange natural phenomena as earthquakes and eclipses. They believed that these phenomena were caused by a most powerful supernatural force, which was invisible and intangible. Likewise, in human affairs there were successes and failures, gains and losses, which were unpredictable or uncontrollable. Men could only find explanations for them in the will of Heaven or in destiny.

Confucius believed in the will of Heaven. He said,

At fifty I understood the will of Heaven(2.4).

The gentleman stands in awe of three things: the will of Heaven, great men, and the words of the sages. The small man does not stand in awe of the will of Heaven, for he does not know of it; he despises great men, and ridicules the words of the sages.

(16.8)

By "great men" is meant men of high position. Confucius not only believed in the will of Heaven, but considered those who did not understand and therefore did not fear and revere it as "small men."

From some of his remarks we can deduce how Confucius looked at the will of Heaven or destiny. Once in Kuang he was mistaken for someone else and detained; he was in great danger. He then proclaimed,

> **As King Wen has died, is all the cultural heritage not kept in me? If Heaven had desired its extinction, I would not have acquired it. If Heaven does not desire its extinction, what harm can the men of Kuang do to me? (9.5)**

What he meant by this is quite clear. He believed it was his mission, after King Wen, King Wu and the Duke of Zhou, to promote and enact the social institutions and political system of the Western Zhou, and this mission was given him by Heaven. Because of this belief he had courage and confidence, and never feared or wavered in the face of difficulties and dangers.

Despite this, the ideal of humane government, for which Confucius strove all his life, was not realized. Since he had no doubt about the correctness of his views, he could only presume that it was destiny that had failed him:

It is destiny if the Way is carried out; it is also destiny if the Way is cast away. (14.36)

And only Heaven understood him:

Confucius said, "No one understands me." Zi Gong said, "How is it that no one understands you?" Confucius said, "I do not complain about Heaven; I do not blame men. I study worldly things and try to acquire the highest knowledge. Perhaps only Heaven understands me." (14.35)

In short, Heaven had given him wisdom, virtue and ideals, and he considered that he should dedicate himself to the realization of those ideals. Heaven would decide whether he was to succeed or fail, and it would be pointless to complain about Heaven or to blame men if he failed. The will of Heaven was hard to comprehend but impossible to resist.

Although the will of Heaven decided everything, men should never relax their efforts. All his life Confucius believed that he should "work and learn unflaggingly and teach and enlighten tirelessly," (7.34) and he travelled far and wide to appeal to state rulers to change the chaotic situation there was. The many disappointments, setbacks, difficulties and perils he encountered might have overwhelmed anyone else but were not enough to daunt him. He continued to propagate the Way even in his last years, when he was in his seventies. Just as the gatekeeper at Shimen commented, he was a man who "wants to do what he knows to be impossible." (14.38) This is a very good description of the magnificent spirit Confucius exhibited in his ceaseless struggle. For him, understanding the will of Heaven and striving for his ideals were not contradictory but rather complementary imperatives. He apparently considered his struggle to be the will of Heaven.

天　命

在两千多年前,人们相信上天或上帝决定和控制一切人和事,本来是很自然的。那时人们没有足够的科学知识来解释许多奇怪的自然现象,如地震和日蚀,只得假定有一种看不见、摸不着的巨大的超自然的力量使这些现象发生。人事上的许多预料不到或无法控制的成败得失,也使得人们在天命或命运里找原因。

孔子是相信天命的。他说:

五十而知天命。(2.4)

君子有三畏:畏天命,畏大人,畏圣人之言。小人不知天命而不畏也,狎大人,侮圣人之言。(16.8)

"畏"是敬畏的意思;"大人"指地位高的人。孔子不仅相信天命,而且认为只有小人才不懂得因而也就不敬畏天命。

从他说的一些话中可以大体看出他怎样理解天命或命运。有一次他在匡这个地方被当地人认错并拘禁起来,情况十分危急。这时他说:

文王既没,文不在兹乎? 天之将丧斯文也,后死者不得与于斯文也; 天之未丧斯文也,匡人其如

予何？（9.5）

（周文王已经死了，典章制度不就在我这里吗？天若是要使它失传，我这个后死的人就不会掌握它了；天若是不愿使它失传，匡人又能把我怎么样呢？）

这几句话的意思很清楚：孔子认为继文、武、周公之后传布并推行西周的典章制度是他的使命，而这个使命是上天授予他的。这个信念给他勇气和信心，使他在任何艰难危险面前毫不畏惧与动摇。

然而孔子毕生为之奋斗的、推行仁政的理想并没有实现。他对自己思想的正确是不会怀疑的，所以他只能假定使他失败的是命运了：

道之将行也与，命也；道之将废也与，命也。（14.36）

而了解他的只有上天：

子曰："莫我知也夫。"子贡曰："何为其莫知子也？"子曰："不怨天，不尤人，下学而上达。知我者其天乎。"（14.35）

（孔子说："没有人知道我了。"子贡说："为什么没有人知道先生呢？"孔子说："我不埋怨天，也不责备人，我学习人间的事理，逐渐明白天命。知道我的只有天了。"）

总之，是上天给他智慧、品德与理想，他应该为实现理想而献身。他的成败也是上天决定的，所以失败了也不必怨天尤人。天命难以解释，但不可抗拒。

　　固然天命在主宰一切，但人的努力不可放松。孔子一生"为之不厌，诲人不倦"(7.34)，为改变那混乱的局势奔走呼吁。他所遭受的那些失望与挫折，艰难与危险，足以压倒任何别的人，但并没有使他悲观丧气。到七十高龄他仍然继续传播他的道。诚如石门的守门人所说，孔子是"知其不可为而为之者。"(14.38) 这句话说出了孔子的伟大的奋斗精神。对他来说，知天命与奋斗并不是矛盾的，而是一致的。可能他认为奋斗也是天命。

Ghosts and Spirits

In Confucius' day it was generally believed that ghosts and spirits not only existed but had a mysterious power over the fate of the living. Neither Confucius, nor anyone else, however, had sufficient knowledge or evidence to disprove this belief. Therefore Confucius wisely advised his students not to spend time on this question; instead, he counselled, they had better deal with the real world:

Ji Lu talked about serving ghosts and spirits. Confucius said, "How can one serve ghosts and spirits before one knows how to serve men?" "May I ask about death?" The answer was: "How can one understand death before one understands life?" (11.12)

Fan Chi asked about wisdom. Confucius said, "To work for the common people's reasonable needs and keep one's distance from but show reverence to ghosts and spirits may be what wisdom means." (6.22)

In answering Ji Lu (Zi Lu), Confucius said that it was more important to serve the living than to serve (to offer sacrifices to) ghosts and spirits, and that it was more important to understand life than to make guesses about what would happen to one after death. In answering Fan Chi, Confucius pointed out that it was wise to work for the common people's reasonable needs and not to bother about ghosts and spirits. Obviously, Confucius was, and advised his students to be, more concerned with man and life than with ghosts and spirits, or with things after death.

These views were important because in Confucius' time people, especially the rulers, were very superstitious, and would do or not do things merely for fear of offending ghosts and spirits. There were officials who conducted large-scale sacrificial ceremonies in honor of ghosts and spirits while neglecting things they ought to do for the benefit of the people. That is probably why Confucius urged Fan Chi "to work for the common people's reasonable needs."

These views proved Confucius to be a realist. His practical and realistic spirit was to profoundly influence the Chinese people's outlook on life.

鬼 神

在孔子那个时代，人们普遍相信鬼神是存在的，而且有种神秘的力量足以影响活人的命运。孔子并没有——任何人都不可能有——足够的知识或证据来否定它们的存在。但孔子明智地劝他的弟子不必研究这个问题，还是面对现实世界为好：

季路问事鬼神。子曰："未能事人，焉能事鬼？"曰："敢问死。"曰："未知生，焉知死？"（11.12）

樊迟问知。子曰："务民之义，敬鬼神而远之，可谓知矣。"（6.22）

在答复季路（即子路）时，孔子强调奉事活人（为活人服务）比奉事鬼神（祭祀鬼神）重要，懂得生活比猜测死后的事重要。在答复樊迟时，孔子指出，能够为民众的合理的、正当的需要工作，就可算是聪明；至于鬼神，应该敬而远之，不必时常想到或为之做点什么，还是要把为民众做事放在前面。在后一个答复中，孔子用"民"字，可见是为从政者着想的。有的从政者在祭祀鬼神上大做文章，而把民众的事放在脑后，这就愚蠢了。

孔子关于鬼神的观点证明他是个现实主义者，他关心的是人，是生活，不是鬼神或死后的事。这个观点对以后的中国人的人生观有重大的影响。

The Mean

One gem of Confucius' philosophy is the theory of *zhongyong*, or the mean. The term appears only once in *The Analects*:

Confucius said, "*Zhonyong* should be a perfect virtue. The common people have been short of it for a long time." (6.29)

But the theory underlines quite a few other remarks of Confucius, who apparently wanted his students to take it as a guide to action and thinking.

Zhong means middle, not leaning to one side, neither going too far nor falling short; *yong* means ordinary. So *zhongyong* is the opposite of extremism, excess, one-sidedness, departure from the normal. Its English equivalent may be "the mean."

An examination of natural phenomena, social reality and human life would reveal to the observer that the most ideal state, quality, relationship, or measure is the mean. Examples abound: excessively hot or cold weather; excessively dry or wet places; the presence of unlimited personal freedom or the total absence of freedom in social life; gluttony or eating nothing; one's size or weight being too big or too small — these excesses would cause trouble or damage, upset the balance, even change the original nature of things.

It is perhaps common sense that, when one deals with a problem, one needs to be on guard against going too far or not far enough; against being too harsh or too weak. The middle way is generally desirable — that is, the way in accordance with the doctrine of the mean.

Confucius often taught his students to act and behave according to the principle of the mean. In the previous section on education this was illustrated when he said about two of his students: "Qiu tends to hold back, so I tried to urge him forward; You has the courage of two men, so I tried to hold him back." This shows that he did not approve of people shrinking before problems, nor did he approve of acting rashly.

In the following dialogue Confucius put forward a very important principle:

> **Zi Gong asked, "Who is better, Shi or Shang?" Confucius said, "Shi goes too far, and Shang falls short." "Is Shi better then?" Confucius said, "Going too far is the same as falling short." (11.16)**

Shi and Shang were two of Confucius' disciples. According to the master, going too far and falling short are equally wrong, because neither conforms to the principle of the mean. Those who believe going too far is better may overdo things and invariably end up incurring losses or making mistakes.

The Chinese maxim "A person should be both simple and refined" contains an element of the doctrine of the mean. Simplicity and refinement are conflicting qualities. Possessing one without the other would lead to a bad result. Confucius said,

He who shows more simplicity than refinement is rude; he who shows more refinement than simplicity is like an office clerk. Only a proper blending of these two factors makes a gentleman. (6.18)

So the ideal state is one where there is both simplicity and refinement, with neither quality dominant, that is, in the state of the mean.

The above quotations may help us to understand why Confucius said that the mean is a "perfect virtue." In one's conduct and in one's dealings with others, to adhere to the principle of the mean should be the best approach.

In fact, ordinary people often do things in accordance with the principle of the mean, though they are ignorant of the philosophy. This principle can be seen everywhere as it is applicable everywhere. It is both common and valuable. This, perhaps, is what *yong* (ordinary) means. When he said that the common people had been short of it for a long time, Confucius may have meant that during the chaotic Spring and Autumn Period many people had lost this ordinary virtue.

中　庸

在《论语》中孔子用"中庸"这一名词只有一次:

中庸之为德也,其至矣乎! 民鲜久矣。(6. 29)

(中庸该是最完美的道德了! 人们缺少它已经很久了。)

中庸是什么意思? 它为什么是完美的道德? 这是我们所要讨论的问题。

"中"就是中间,不偏不倚,不过头也不是不及;"庸"就是平常。与中庸相反的是极端、过分、片面、反常。

如果我们观察自然现象、社会现实,或个人生活,我们会发现中庸是最佳的状态、品质、关系,或措施。例如天气的太冷或太热,地方的太干或太湿;社会生活的无限制的自由或完全没有自由,法律的过严或过松,一个人身材过胖或过瘦,饮食过多或过少,等等,都会引起问题,造成损失,失去平衡,甚至改变事物的本来性质。

常识告诉我们,在处理一个问题时,需要警惕不要做得过分,也不要做得太少;不要太强硬、太苛刻,也不要太软弱、太宽大。适中总是可取的。所谓适中,就是符合中庸之道。

　　孔子常常教导他的学生按中庸的原则办事。我们在论教育一章中引过孔子说的"求也退，故进之；由也兼人，故退之"一段话，可见孔子既不赞成遇事退缩，也不赞成做事过头。

　　在下面的谈话中，孔子提出了一个重要的原则：

　　子贡问："师与商也孰贤？"子曰："师也过，商也不及。"曰："然则师愈与？"子曰："过犹不及。"（11．16）

　　（子贡问道："子张和子夏谁强一些？"孔子说："子张往往过分，子夏往往差一步。"子贡说："那么子张强些了？"孔子说："过分和差一步是同样的。"）

　　"过"和"不及"都不是中庸，所以都不对。那些认为过比不及好的人做事往往过头，结果总是与愿望相反，造成损失或错误。

　　我们常说的"文质彬彬"的原义也包含中庸的因素。孔子说：

　　质胜文则野，文胜质则史。文质彬彬，然后君子。（6．18）

　　（朴实胜过文采，就会粗野。文采胜过朴实，就会像文书官。只有文采和朴实适当结合，才成为一个君子。）

　　朴实和文采是相反的品质，如走极端，只要其中的一项，效果就不好。理想的情况是既朴实又有文采，并且在两方面都不过分。这也就是中庸的状态。

　　上面引的孔子的话可以帮助我们理解为什么中庸是种完美的道德。为人处事应防止过分与不及，避免片面与极端，坚持中庸的原则。

　　事实上，民众在日常生活中，尽管不知道中庸的哲理，却经常按照中庸的道理办事。中庸的道理随处可见，到处可用，十分平凡，而又十分宝贵。这就是"庸"字的意思。孔子说"民鲜久矣"，可能是指在那乱世，许多人连这个常见常有的道理都丧失了。

Harmony

The mean brings about harmony. In this regard, the relationship between simplicity and refinement is instructive. If a person has only one of the two qualities, he is either simple or refined, and that is not an ideal state. If the principle of the mean is followed, he may combine the two qualities into a harmonious, integrated whole, with neither quality in excess, and that is an ideal state.

Confucius valued harmony:

The gentleman aims at harmony, not uniformity; the small man prefers uniformity, not harmony. (13.23)

The gentleman favors a world in which a multiplicity of diverse views and phenomena exist in harmony, while the small man demands uniformity or unanimity. Two analogies respecting cooking and music had been made before Confucius' time to illustrate the importance of the principle of harmony: different ingredients make a tasty dish, and a variety of musical instruments produce beautiful music. Harmony presupposes difference.

Moreover, harmony is a fundamental principle of

human society and nature. Society is made up of all kinds of people who have a great variety of views and activities , but must co-exist. For this to occur, both difference and harmony are necessary.

You Zi, one of Confucius' disciples, said,

The most valuable thing brought about by the use of the rites is harmony. (1.12)

The rites, as regulations governing people's conduct, while to ordinary people they seemed to have a restraining or limiting function only, were in You Zi's view the best means to promote harmony. This view shows You Zi's admirable insight, for restraint and limitations prevented improper or undue behavior, thus making it easy for people to live harmoniously together.

Just as human society is made up of all kinds of people, so is nature composed of myriad things, which are all different. There would be no nature if this diversity were not present. At the same time, all these things, generally speaking, exist in harmony. The major underlying principle in nature is harmony in diversity. Without harmony, nature would destroy itself.

The Doctrine of the Mean contains the following statement:

The mean is the great foundation, and harmony is the ultimate principle, of the

universe. As the mean and harmony are attained, heaven and earth are in their proper places, and all things are nourished.

Ancient Chinese philosophers understood that all the things in the universe are inter-connected in one way or another, and thanks to the principles of the mean and harmony, they exist and grow.

和　谐

中庸导致和谐。就上面提到的质与文的关系来说，如果只取其一，结果便是单一的质或单一的文。如果采取中庸的路线，把质和文恰当地结合起来，这两种因素便可构成一个和谐的整体。很明显，单一的状态并不完美，两种因素和谐地结合才是完美的。所以孔子说：

君子和而不同，小人同而不和。(13.23)

"和"是和谐，"同"是一律。君子愿意看到不同的事物、观点、因素和谐相处，小人则强求一律。古人曾以做菜和音乐为例来说明和的重要：油、盐、酱、醋各种口味的材料混合到一起，才能做成美味的食物；各种乐器的音色不同的声音融合在一起才能构成悦耳的音乐。可见和是以不同为前提的。

和是人类社会，也是自然界的一个基本原则。社会是各种各样的人组成的，他们的思想与活动各不相同，但他们又必须生活在一起。所以社会要存在和发展，既需要不同，也需要和谐。

孔子的弟子有子说：

礼之用，和为贵。(2.12)

礼本来是关于人的行为的各种规定，似乎只是起约束、限制的作用。但有子认为礼的作用在于促进和谐，这是很有见地的，因为约束和限制阻止了过分的或不恰当的行为，从而使人们易于和谐相处。

同样，自然界是由数不清的千差万别的东西构成的。如果只有一种东西，那也就没有我们所知的自然界了。同时这些数不清的东西，总的说来，也是和谐相处的。如果不是这样，自然界会毁灭它自己。

《中庸》里有这样一段话：

中也者，天下之大本也；和也者，天下之达道也。致中和，天地位焉，万物育焉。

（中是天下的最大的根本，和是天下的普遍的原则。中与和的道理实现了，天与地就各得其所，万物就生长了。）

古人早就看到，宇宙间的万物彼此都有某种联系，是中庸与和谐的原则使它们可能存在和生长。

Knowledge and Practice

One of Confucius' pronouncements regarding knowledge is particularly important in illustrating its complex nature:

You know what you know; you do not know what you do not. That is knowledge. (2.17)

The meaning of this saying may be understood from two perspectives. On the one hand, one's correct attitude to knowledge consists in stating that one knows certain things while being ignorant of many others. In other words, one should be honest in regard to knowledge, and should not profess to know what one really does not . Assuming such an attitude, one will be able to acquire new and genuine knowledge.

On the other hand, one's knowledge is finite. Many things are accessible to one, while many other things are not. A person who studies and explores earnestly may add something to the total store of human knowledge, but it is impossible for anyone to ever know everything. An appreciation of this reality forces one to appraise one's knowledge objectively, prevents self-complacency, and compels one to be modest about one's own knowledge and yet eager to learn.

What is the purpose of learning? To this question Confucius had a clear answer:

> **What is the use of being able to recite the three hundred songs if one cannot perform the official duties given to one, or negotiate properly when sent to other states? (13.5)**

The three hundred songs refer to those in *The Book of Songs*. During the Spring and Autumn Period, this book was required reading by all government officials, especially negotiators. The 305 songs in it (Confucius said 300 in round figures) touch on facts and thoughts about government, society, custom, history and many other fields. They proved to be helpful to officials and negotiators who could quote lines from the songs to express their ideas. When Confucius asked what use there was in studying the book if one could not perform one's official duties or negotiate properly, he meant that one should study the book in order to use it in one's work, and that being unable to use it amounted to not having studied it.

With regard to the relationship between knowledge and practice, this saying implies that knowledge should be integrated with practice, and that practice is the purpose and test of knowledge.

When Confucius talked about learning or
knowledge, his main concern was obviously the
learning and knowledge of the Way — the way of
cultivating oneself, regulating the family, governing
the state, and pacifying the country. It is clear that
one learns these ways only for the purpose of
practicing them, and practicing them whole-
heartedly, happily, with an urge that cannot be
swerved. Confucius said,

> **Knowing [the Way] is not so good as liking
> it; liking it is not so good as finding joy in
> it. (6.20)**

All his life Confucius learned and taught tirelessly;
when he was busy working, he sometimes forgot to
eat; and when he was happy, he would forget his
worries. He was a man who found joy in the Way.

Finally a mention of Confucius' views on speech
and action. He said,

> **The gentleman is inclined to be slow in
> speech but quick in action. (4.24)**
> **The gentleman considers it a shame to
> talk more than he does. (14.27)**
> **The gentleman acts before he talks, and
> then talks according to what he does. (2.13)**

These sayings are similar in meaning: it is good
to talk little but do much, and act before talking.
Speech relates to action in the same way as

knowledge relates to practice: what is important is action or practice.

知　行

关于知的意义，孔子说了一句很重要的话：

> 知之为知之，不知为不知，是知也。(2. 17)

这句话的意思可分两个层次来理解。知道的就是知道的，不知道的就是不知道的，这才是对知的正确态度。换言之，在知识问题上要有个实事求是，也就是老实的态度，不要强不知以为知。只有这样，才能不断取得新的真正的知识。这是第一层意思。

但一个人的知识是有限度的：许多事物是可知的，也有许多事物是不可知的，现在不知道，将来也不会知道。一个认真探索研究的人会在人类知识的总和上添加一点新的东西，但任何人都不可能认识一切事物，掌握一切知识。有了这个认识，人就会客观地评价自己的知识，不会盲目自满，而会谦虚好学。这是第二层意思。

从上述两个方面去理解这句话，对于求知的人是很有益处的。求知的目的何在？对这个问题孔子有明确的观点：

> 诵诗三百，授之以政，不达；使于四方，不能专对；虽多，亦奚以为？ (13. 5)
> （诵读《诗经》三百首诗，让他办理政事，却办

**不成；让他出使各地，不能独立地谈话应对；虽
然学得多，有什么用呢？）**

在春秋时期，《诗经》这本书是从政者，尤其是
使臣必读的书。这本书中的三百零五首诗（这里说
"三百"，是说一整数）涉及到政治、社会、民风、历
史等许多方面的情况和道理，学好了应该有助于从
政，更有助于谈判，因为可以引用诗句来表达各种意
思。孔子说，学了《诗经》而仍然不能办理政事或谈
判，那学了有什么用？意思就是学是为了用，用不上
等于没有学。

联系知行的关系来看，孔子这句话的意思是知与
行应该结合，知是为了行，行检验知。

孔子谈学或知，主要是指学道或知道，即修身、
齐家、治国、平天下的道理。学这些道理，目的当然
更是在于行，而且是出自内心的、愉快的、欲罢不能
的行：

知之者不如好之者，好之者不如乐之者。(6.20)
**（知道［道］的人不如爱好它的人，爱好它的人
不如以它为乐的人。）**

孔子一生"为之不厌，诲人不倦"，"发愤忘食，
乐以忘忧"，体现了"乐之者"的精神。

再提一下孔子对言与行的关系的看法。他说：

君子欲讷于言而敏于行。(4.24)
君子耻其言而过其行。(14.27)
［君子］先行其言而后从之。(2.13)

这三句话的意思相近：说话要迟缓些，行动要敏捷些；要以说得多、做得少为耻；先把自己要说的话做出来，然后再照做的说。总之，要少说多做，先做后说。言行的关系和知行的关系相同：重要的是行。

Chapter Eight: Confucius' Influence

Confucius had an incomparably extensive, profound, and lasting influence on Chinese society. From 140 B.C. when Emperor Wudi of the Han dynasty decided, on the recommendation of Dong Zhongshu, to make Confucianism the orthodox philosophy and exclude scholars of all other schools from the civil service, to the founding of the People's Republic (1949), excluding a few short periods like the Wei and Jin dynasties, Confucianism was the mainstream of Chinese thought. Throughout this long period the thinking and behavior of people from all levels of society, from emperors and ministers to peasants and craftsmen, were invariably permeated with Confucianism. Whether in court politics or in the daily life of the common people, signs of his influence could be seen everywhere.

Confucius said that he would rather transmit than create and that he had a liking for the ancients. He inherited the thought of ancient sages, especially that of the founders of the Western Zhou. After him there were in nearly every dynasty scholars who tried to interpret and develop his philosophy. These scholars formed the powerful Confucian school. Their views, however, are not entirely identical with those of Confucius, the founder of the school, for many of them had new views and theories, which Confucius never touched upon. Confucius never said, for instance, "If the emperor wants a minister to die, the minister dare not keep himself alive;" nor did he ever advocate women's "three obediences and four virtues,"* though these were generally believed to be Confucian tenets. The present discussion of his influence confines itself to his views alone, and the influence of later Confucian scholars, whether positive or negative, will not be included.

---

*An ethical code that required women to obey their fathers, husbands and sons, and to attend to morality, way of speech, appearance, and work.

There are two principal aspects of his influence: that which deals with the academic or theoretical field and that which concerns social life. His influence on scholars like Mencius and Xun Qing of the Warring States Period, Dong Zhongshu of the Han dynasty, and many others, including some contemporary philosophers, is clear. However, since there have been intensive discussions of these thinkers in works on the history of Chinese philosophy, they are not dealt with here. Only his influence on social life will be discussed in this chapter. By social life we mean people's behavior and conduct, values, inter-personal relations, family life, and economic and political activities. It is in these aspects of social life in particular where the pervasive influence that Confucius exerted over Chinese society can be seen most clearly. A few examples of it will be given here.

Confucius laid great stress on the necessity of moral cultivation, and hoped that everyone would become a virtuous gentleman or good man. This idea, propagated by scholars and students of the classics of every generation, was generally accepted. The moral criteria outlined in Confucian thought were accepted by the majority of the Chinese people as the standards whereby right was distinguished from wrong. They accordingly believed that they should behave in a moral fashion only, and eschew the immoral, and that anyone who did something immoral was sure to be blamed and condemned, and bring shame on himself. This does not mean that there were no wicked people, but they were always in the minority.

Although China was a country having a large geographical area and a vast population, and the government was a huge, complex and many-layered bureaucratic structure, in normal times government functioned effectively. This was not because there were many laws and regulations to unify people's actions. In fact, there was never anything in Chinese history that could be called a constitution, and even other laws were few in number. There were no local law-courts or police forces, and not many scholars or people of other circles were interested in the study of law. The successful conduct of government work and maintenance of order relied mainly, therefore, on the moral sense of the majority of the officials and common people, most of whom valued moral principles, adhered to them, accepting them as the supreme rules for government.

As a rule, people were evaluated by moral standards: there were loyal and disloyal ministers, upright and corrupt officials, filial and unfilial sons, righteous heroes and evil brigands, and so on. When people talked about the popular *Romance of the Three Kingdoms*, they would praise good characters like Zhuge Liang and Guan Yu, and curse bad ones like Dong Zhuo and Cao Cao. In the eyes of the ordinary people, characters of dramas were categorized into good ones and bad ones, according to moral standards.

Ancient heroes were primarily virtuous people. They either dedicated their lives to the cause of the country or the service of the people, or fought to death against evil forces with unbending determination, or gave their lives in battle against foreign invaders. They epitomized what Confucius said about humane men sacrificing their lives to realize humanity. Historical records are full of such great people, who were unreservedly respected. They showed the great strength of morality.

Rule of the country and maintenance of order depended, as well, on customs and habits passed down from generation to generation. When a problem arose, officials and common people alike would first recall how their fathers or grandfathers, or even ancestors, had dealt with a similar problem, and then they thought they had elicited guidelines for the solution. Such a habitual and traditional approach to problems was not very different from that of the function of the rites which Confucius emphasized. As we have seen, he was opposed to guiding the people with government orders and regulating them with penalties, while advocating guiding them with virtue and regulating them with the rites. For about 2,000 years this principle was to a certain extent followed, only the rites of the Zhou were replaced by later social traditions, customs and habits.

Confucius tried hard to revive the Zhou rites, regarding them as a panacea for the chaotic situation of his day. In fact, this view was not only conservative, but retrogressive, and had no prospect of being realized. The confusion of the Spring and Autumn Period was itself proof that the Zhou rites were out of keeping with the changing society, which was crying out for a new system. Because he failed to recognize this fact, he put forward proposals that were doomed to fail. Later traditions and customs, while helping to maintain social stability, gradually turned into conservative forces, forces that slowed down and even stifled the growth of new ideas and new systems. The enduring stability of China's feudal society brought with it one serious effect — lasting stagnation. Social development was extremely slow. There was no revolutionary change in the social, economic or political system for 2,000 years. This was connected with the stabilizing and restraining role of social traditions.

Social stability was also related to Confucius' belief in the doctrine of the mean and his stress upon the importance of harmony. Under his influence, all people, especially the educated, tended to avoid going to extremes and confrontation. Confucius also taught that one should seek whatever one needed in oneself, not in others (15.21), and that, when trouble occurred, one should blame oneself more than others (15.15). As a result, forbearance was considered a virtue. All this played its part, ideologically, as a factor in the promotion of peace and social stability.

Humane government and rule by virtue, which Confucius preached in all earnestness, were not accepted by any ruler during his lifetime. In addition, after his death, there was hardly any emperor dedicated to these ideals, though many professed a belief in Confucius' thought. However, in spite of this, on certain sensible or clear-headed emperors these ideals had a restrictive effect, preventing them from oppressing and exploiting the people too harshly. It was also true that in every dynasty a few good ministers and other officials, who sincerely believed in Confucius' instructions, worked for the people's benefit.

Confucius' theory of government had a fatal flaw

in that it advocated pinning all the hope for humane government and rule by virtue on the ruler alone. Since few rulers were virtuous, his effort was fruitless. In his view the main political problem of the time was the seizure of power by noble houses or vassals of low ranks. Because of this he urged all the nobles to be loyal and obedient to their prince or king, but offered no mechanism to induce the ruler to practice humane government. He failed to appreciate the strength of the common people. They were to the ruler, provided he was virtuous, what grass was to wind: grass would bend when wind was blowing. The people had to obey whatever orders he might give. His words "The common people should be made to follow orders, not to understand them" (8.9) also revealed his distrust of the people. Confucius had no democratic ideas. Perhaps it was impossible for democratic ideas to arise in his time. In any case, autocracy in feudal China was strengthened by the commonly accepted tenet that all subjects should be loyal to the ruler and the lack of democratic ideas.

Confucius stressed the importance of filial piety and respect for brothers, considering them the two prime virtues that all young people should acquire. His disciple You Zi went a step further by saying that these two virtues were "the root of humanity."

These teachings greatly influenced the Chinese people's attitude towards the family. The Chinese probably attached greater importance to the family and showed greater respect to their fathers and elder brothers than many other peoples. In the past the Chinese had a special liking for the big family — people of several generations living in one house. Whether the family was big or small, the patriarch had an indisputable authority over the other members, who had to obey him, at least ostensibly so.

Women had a much lower standing in the family than men. Confucius once said something to show his disdain for women (17.25), and this remark was to have a deleterious influence on both men and women in later ages. But some later Confucian scholars went even further and devised many rules discriminating against women, making them live with their heads bowed all their lives.

The Chinese not only set great store by the family, but by the clan. This attitude may have originated in the clan system that had existed long before Confucius, but it had some connection with his advocacy of filial piety and brotherly respect. In rural areas it was common for people of the same clan to live close together, form a community, trace their line of descent, set up a clan temple, and elect a clan head, usually an old and rich landlord, of a higher generation. He or other important men of the clan had the right to settle disputes between clansmen.

The old people, who had the final say in the family or the clan, always followed established customs when there were problems to deal with and were opposed to departing from tradition. This added to the force of conservatism and stability in Chinese society.

But the family also played a positive role in Chinese society. A person spent all his life in the family. He was brought up and educated in the family when he was young, and supported and looked after when he was old. He could expect help from his family whenever he met with difficulties or fell ill. The family prevented loneliness and all the problems that came with it, and greatly reduced the burden of the community.

People's attachment to the family was extended to their home region. In the past only a small proportion of Chinese ever left their birthplaces to travel to other places. This was especially true of people in rural areas. Those who had to leave their home towns would try hard to return there when they were old. The proverb "When leaves fall, they fall near the root of the tree" reflects this feeling.

The reluctance to move was mainly the result of small-scale farming and transport conditions, but people's mentality was also an important cause. Filial piety required sons to stay at home to look after their parents. Confucius said, "One should not travel far while his parents are alive; if one has to, one should keep them informed of his whereabouts." (4.19)

Those who spent all their lives in one place naturally had a very limited knowledge of the world, and it was not easy for them to get in touch with new ideas. This was also a factor in their conservative tendency.

All his life Confucius was engaged in education, teaching and training people who would carry on his mission. In later times, since he was regarded as a sage and since his teachings were taken as the criteria distinguishing right from wrong, education and study were considered most important by people of all circles and all strata. This belief had a great historic significance: it helped to advance the culture of China. Before the eighteenth century Chinese culture was one of the greatest in the world, and it was Confucius' influence that made this possible.

The modern Chinese educational system had its beginnings in the first years of the present century. Until then there were no primary or middle schools such as they are today, but countless *sishu*, or private schools, were scattered over the country. In such schools there was only one teacher who taught students of different age groups in one classroom. Small children learned to read and write, and older ones began to read the classics and well-known essays and poems, the *Four Books** being the basic material. Building on this foundation, those favored by economic and other conditions would continue to study the classics to prepare themselves for the imperial examinations and the civil service.

The well educated commanded respect and enjoyed a high social status, partly because they possessed a great deal of knowledge, and partly because they had the prospect of entering the ranks of officials. When people talked about professions, they would say "scholars, peasants, craftsmen and merchants," with scholars leading the list. Teaching was an honorable profession, and the teacher was very much respected by his students and their parents. On the wall of the central hall of many homes, written on paper or wood, were these five words: "Heaven, Earth, Emperor, Parents and Teacher," and on festivals the whole family would

---

*The *Four Books* are *The Analects, The Mencius, The Great Learning,* and *The Doctrine of the Mean.*

burn incense and bow to them.

Although it was not impossible for children of poor families to study and become officials, most of those who adopted this career were the children of rich people, in the main landlords. Because of their family's wealth, they did not have to work and could concentrate on their studies, if they wanted to. So most scholars were in fact part of the landlord class. They were brought up in, and in turn spread, Confucian ideas, influencing the thinking and behavior of the public, and at certain periods of history they were a contributing factor to the stability of Chinese society.

Confucius urged his students to study the Way, as opposed to learning any techniques. In his day this orientation may have been reasonable, for wars, political upheavals and social instability demanded immediate attention. But scholars of later ages, despite the changed situation, still focused their efforts on literature, history and philosophy, and made working in the government their main objective. As a result, they showed little interest in science and technology. The many scientists and inventors China produced in the past must have disregarded Confucius' dislike of specific skills.

All in all, Confucius' influence on education in China was in the main positive, though it contained some negative elements.

Born in a period of disorder and confusion, Confucius devoted all his life to the cause of restoring order and normality. He was preoccupied with the pressing issues of the day, and gave very little attention to other questions, especially unreal ones. Demons and gods were among the things he seldom talked about (7.21), and he advised his disciples not to speculate on what ghosts and spirits might do and what would happen after death (11.12). In other words, he was mainly concerned with reality and life. This practical and down-to-earth spirit was to play an important part in shaping the Chinese national character and the qualities of Chinese culture. One obvious expression of it is the fact that few Chinese had any religious belief, let alone religious fervor.

In the first years of the Eastern Han dynasty, at the beginning of the Christian era, Buddhism was introduced into China. During the four or five centuries that followed it gradually spread in the country and it prospered during the Southern and Northern Dynasties of the fifth and sixth centuries. At the same time it was subject to constant criticism. During the Tang dynasty some Buddhist sects were still popular, but beginning with the Song dynasty (after the tenth century) they began to decline.

Although there were a great number of Buddhist temples in the country, real believers constituted only a very small part of the population.

Those who rejected and criticized Buddhism most resolutely were as a rule Confucianists. Upholding the principles laid down by Confucius, they advocated loyalty and filial piety, humanity and rightness; everyone had a duty to serve their ruler and family, and should have a sense of responsibility when the state was in danger or when the populace was suffering. Their practical and worldly outlook was diametrically opposite to that of the Buddhists, who considered the world illusory. It was natural, therefore, that they should be opposed to Buddhism.

The Taoist religion*, founded by Chinese, preached quietism and nonaction. So it also contradicted Confucian doctrines and was bitterly opposed by the Confucianists.

During the 2,000 years from the Eastern Han to the Qing dynasty, neither the Buddhist nor the Taoist religion ever overwhelmed Confucianism to become the dominant school of thought, a testimony to the incomparable power of the latter. It possessed

---

*The Taoist religion is different from Taoism as a philosophy. The religion combines some elements of the philosophy with mysticism and the worship of many gods.

this power because it met the needs of China's feudal society and was rooted in the minds of the people.

Many countries have been troubled by religious wars, but China has never seen one.

The view has been advanced that Confucianism is also a religion, just like the Buddhist and Taoist religions; hence there were three religions in China.

Confucius' thought, if we consider its pervasive and lasting influence, is really similar to a religion. But to call Confucius the founder of a religion would be inappropriate, for there are essential differences between them.

The founder of a religion either claims to be or is regarded as a prophet speaking on behalf of God; he is different from an ordinary man. Conveying God's wishes, he teaches people to believe in God or gods, and advises them to do good; if so, they may go to Heaven after death; if not, they may end up in Hell. He establishes a religious organization, with elaborate rituals and regulations.

Confucius was not such a man. He said of himself, "I was a humble man when young;" (9.6) "I was not born with knowledge, but I am fond of antiquity and quick in seeking knowledge;" (7.20) and "How dare I be called a sage or a humane man?" (7.34) In short, he considered himself an ordinary man, not a representative of God.

What he taught was not God's wishes, but truths based on real life that intended to solve concrete problems. He aimed to raise the moral standard of the ruler as well as the common people, in an attempt to stabilize social order and improve government. He did not teach people to believe in God so as to win happiness in this life or the next. The Chinese of subsequent ages accepted his ideas only because they were correct, applicable, and beneficial to everyone who wanted to be an upright man.

In every age after Confucius there have been Confucian scholars who worked hard to propagate his thought, but there has never been a religious organization with Confucius as its god or prophet.

Today there seems to be a revival of Confucius' influence not only in China, but in many other, mainly Asian, countries. People are talking about Confucianism being a factor in the rapid development of some countries and regions in East Asia and an antidote to the many ills of the modern age. This is a new sign of the philosophy's inexhaustible vitality and immeasurable force — a force that resides in its being practical, realistic and down-to-earth.

A scholar of the Song dynasty said, "Had Heaven not produced Zhongni (Confucius), there would be

230 UNDERSTANDING CONFUCIUS 孔子新评

an eternal night." This poetic exaggeration expresses the believers' conviction that Confucius defined what is right and what is wrong so that people would have guidelines to follow and would no longer have to grope blindly in the dark for truths. The correct attitude to his thought is perhaps one of study, analysis, and discrimination: one should accept those ideas that warrant acceptance and reject those ideas that deserve rejection. It is clear that not all his ideas are outdated or outmoded simply because they were propounded 2,500 years ago, and at the sametime, not all are still valid today.

Moral cultivation, education, the doctrine of the mean and harmony, and the practical spirit, all of which Confucius valued, have exerted an enormously powerful influence over the formation of the Chinese character and pushed Chinese culture forward. While his principles of government, his emphasis on the rites, and his attention to family relations have helped to make Chinese society peaceful and stable over long periods, they have at the same time slowed down its change and development.

第八章　　孔子的影响

　　孔子的思想对中国社会的影响无可比拟地广泛、深刻和持久。从汉武帝采纳董仲舒的建议，决定"罢黜百家，独尊儒术"（公元前140年）起，直到1949年新中国建立，除较短时期（魏、晋）外，孔子思想成为中国思想的主流达两千年之久。在这么长的时间里，各阶层的中国人，上自帝王大臣，下到农夫工匠，思想上无不打上孔子学说的烙印。不论宫廷政治还是老百姓的日常生活，处处可见孔子思想的痕迹。

　　孔子说自己"述而不作，信而好古。"他继承了古代，尤其是西周立国人的思想。在他以后，历代都有学者解释和发展他的学说，形成了强大的儒家学派。孔子是儒家学派的创建人，但孔子的思想和后世

的儒家思想并不完全相同,因为许多儒家学者有新的
见解和学说,是孔子没有涉及到的。例如孔子并没有
说过"君叫臣死,臣不敢不死",也没有主张过妇女
的"三从四德"*。我们讨论孔子的影响,应以孔子自
己的观点为依据,不应把后世儒家学者所产生的影
响,不管是积极的还是消极的,统统归之于孔子。

孔子的影响大致可分两个方面:一是对学术界或
理论界的影响,一是对社会生活的影响。从战国时期
的孟轲、荀卿,西汉的董仲舒,一直到当代的一些哲
学家,都受到他的影响。许多哲学史对这一方面都有
详尽的论述,我们在本章里就不再讨论了。社会生活
包括人们的行为举止、价值观念、人际关系、家庭生
活、经济及政治活动,等等。孔子对中国社会的无比
的巨大影响,主要表现在这些方面,我们在本章中将
试图列举几点。

孔子重视道德修养,希望人人都成为有道德的君
子或好人。经过世代读书人的传播,这一思想可以说
被普遍地接受了。多数中国人以孔子拟定的道德标准
作为是非标准;认为符合道德的事可做,不道德的事
不可做,做了就要受到议论和谴责,难以做人。不道
德的人当然总是有的,但毕竟是少数。

---

*"三从"指"未嫁从父,既嫁从夫,夫死从子",要求妇女服从男
权。"四德"指"妇德、妇言、妇容、妇功",要求妇女遵守所谓品德、辞
令、仪态和手艺的"闺范"。

　　中国疆域广大，人口众多，政府机构庞大复杂，层次很多。但在一般情况下，还是实行了有效的治理。这并不是因为有许多法律或规章把人们的行动限制或统一起来。事实上，中国过去并没有一部类似宪法的法律，其他法律也不齐备，没有常设的基层法院或警察，在士农工商各界中没有研究法律的风气。政府工作的进行和社会秩序的维持，主要依靠多数官员和民众的道德观念，他们重视道德，一般遵守道德的要求，把道德看作政治的最高原则。

　　过去评价人物，总是从道德标准出发，如大臣之中有忠臣和奸臣，官员之中有清官和贪官，民众之中有孝子和逆子，义士和恶人，等等。《三国演义》中的诸葛亮和关羽受到普遍的赞美和尊敬，而董卓和曹操便受到责骂。戏曲中的人物，在群众眼中，主要分为好人和坏人，也是按道德标准区分的。

　　历史上许多英雄人物首先是道德高尚的人。他们或是鞠躬尽瘁，为国效劳，为民众做好事；或是与坏人做斗争，大义凛然，宁死不屈；或是抵抗外族入侵，身先士卒，舍身报国。他们做到了孔子说的"无求生以害仁，有杀身以成仁"。这样令人肃然起敬的人物，史不绝书。他们显示了道德的巨大力量。

　　国家的治理和社会秩序的维持，除依靠道德观念外，还有赖于代代相传的风俗习惯。不论政府官员还是老百姓，在处理问题时，往往先回忆父辈、祖父辈，或祖先如何处理类似的问题，这就有章可循了。这种习惯的传统的处理问题的办法，和孔子所强调的礼在性质上相近。孔子不赞成"道之以政，齐之以刑"，而主张"道之以德，齐之以礼"，可以说在很长时间里得到一定程度的实行，只是周礼换成了后来的社会传统和风俗习惯而已。

孔子积极提倡恢复周礼，认为这是整治当时混乱局势的良方，实际上这不止是保守的，而且是倒退的方案，是不可能实现的。春秋时期的混乱正说明周礼已不适应正在变革的社会，这个社会在呼唤新的制度。孔子看不到这一点，因而他的主张注定要失败。以后的社会传统和积习，固然有助于维持社会的稳定，但逐渐变成了保守的力量，在很多时候对新思想、新事物的发展起了阻碍甚至是窒息的作用。中国封建社会长期稳定的后果之一是长期停滞，社会的发展极为缓慢，在两千年中，社会、经济和政治制度没有发生革命性的变革。这与社会传统的稳定和约束作用很有关系。

孔子提倡中庸之道，强调和谐的重要性，受其影响的读书人，以及整个社会，都避免走极端，避免斗争。孔子还教导人凡事要"求诸己"，不要"求诸人"（15．21），遇到问题要"躬自厚而薄责于人"（15．15），就是责己严，责人宽，使得后人以忍让为美德。这些思想原则都有导致社会和平稳定的作用。

孔子大力宣传仁政德治，在他活着的时候，没有哪个统治者接受这个观点。他死后恐怕也没有一个帝王真正做到，尽管不少帝王口头上表示信仰孔子。不过我们也应看到，对一些比较清醒、明智的帝王来说，仁政德治的理想毕竟起了一些约束的作用，使得他们对人民的压迫及剥削不致过分。历代也确实有一些贤臣良吏，真正信奉孔子的教导，为人民谋福利。

孔子在治国的主张上有一个严重的缺陷：把实行仁政德治的希望完全寄托在统治者身上，因而难以收到实效。他认为那时候的主要政治问题是大夫或家臣篡权，所以提倡忠君尊王，没有考虑用什么机制来促使统治者实行仁政。他根本看不到人民群众的力量。在他眼中，正直的统治者和民众的关系是风和草的关系，风吹草倒，统治者发号施令，民众只要服从就行了。"民可使由之，不可使知之"，(8.9)（可以叫民众照上面说的做，而不可使他们知道为什么要那么做）这句话也说明他不相信民众。孔子没有民主思想。也许在他那个时代民主思想是不可能产生的。忠君思想加上民主思想的缺乏助长了中国封建政治的专制性。

孔子重视孝悌，把二者看作年轻人首先要具备的品德。他的门徒有子进一步说孝悌是"仁之本"。这对后世的影响主要表现在家庭观念上。中国人或许比许多其他民族更为重视家庭，更为尊重父兄。过去中国人还特别喜欢几代人同居一宅的大家庭。不论家庭的大小，家长的领导地位是无可争议的，晚辈只能服从，至少也要做到表面服从。

妇女在家庭里的地位比男子为低。孔子说过轻视妇女的话（17.25），对男人和女人的影响都不好。后世一些儒家学者走得更远，立下许多歧视妇女的规矩，使得妇女一辈子抬不起头来。

过去中国人不仅重视家庭，而且重视宗族。这个观念的根源应该是孔子以前的氏族制度，但与孔子提倡孝悌不无关系。在农村，同族人往往聚居在同一个地区，叙辈份，立祠堂，推选族长。族长（一般为年长的、辈份高的、富有的地主）或其他有地位的族人，有权处理本族内的一些纠纷。

在家庭和宗族中，都是长辈或老人主事。他们总是按照老习惯处理问题，反对背离传统，于是又增强了保守和稳定的力量。

但家庭也有很大的积极作用。一个人的一生都是在家庭中度过的。幼年时受到家庭的抚养和教育，老年时受到家庭的赡养和照顾。在任何时候遇到困难或疾病，都可以指望家庭的帮助。这样家庭就使人避免了孤独和孤独带来的种种问题，同时也大大减少了社会的负担。

与重视家庭有关的是重视乡土的思想。过去中国人终身不离开故乡的很多，在农村尤其如此。即使离开了，也设法回来，尤其是年老的时候，此即所谓"叶落归根"。这种情况当然主要是小农生产方式与交通条件造成的，但观念上的原因也很重要。孝道要求人们留在家里奉事父母。孔子也说："父母在，不远游，游必有方。"（4.19）

一辈子生活在一个地方，见闻必然有限，难以受到新的思想的影响，从而助长了人们的保守倾向。

孔子一生办学，教书育人。后世既然尊孔子为圣人，以孔子的是非为是非，自然也就重视教育，提倡读书。这个风气有重大的历史意义，因为它推动了整个中国文化的发展。在十八世纪以前，中国文化是世界文化的一个高峰，这与孔子办学的影响是有关系的。

现有的教育制度从二十世纪初才开始在中国实行。在此以前没有基层的小学和中学，但私塾是相当普遍的。所谓私塾，就是一个教师在一间教室里教年龄不同的学生。儿童学认字和写字，大一点的学生开始学古文，《四书》是基本教材，此外还有些有名的古代诗文。这样打好基础后，有条件的学生再继续钻研古籍，准备参加科举考试，寻求做官的门径。

读书的人受重视，社会地位很高。这一方面因为他们懂得许多道理，一方面因为他们可能做官。过去谈职业，常说"士、农、工、商"，士处于首位。教师是高尚的职业，学生及学生家长非常尊敬他们。许多人家中厅的墙上有一个牌位，上写"天、地、君、亲、师"五个大字，每逢节日，一家人向这个牌位贡香行礼。

贫苦人家的子弟读书做官也是有的，但走这条路的绝大多数人还是富家，主要是地主的子弟。他们的经济条件使得他们不必劳动，只要他们愿意，可以专心读书。所以士实际上是地主阶级的一部分。他们由孔子思想培育起来，以后传播孔子思想，对社会风气有很大的影响，常常是使社会稳定的一个因素。

孔子要求他的学生研究"道"，不要去钻研生产技术。在他那时这个主张也许有一定的道理，因为天下不太平，社会不安定，是首先要解决的问题。但后来的一般读书人，尽管形势已经改变，仍然是只攻文史哲，并以做官为主要目标，对科学技术不感兴趣。中国确实出了许多做出重大贡献的科学家和发明家，他们想必是没有考虑孔子对具体技术的轻视。

总的说来，孔子对后世教育事业的影响是积极的，虽然也有消极的成分。

孔子生于乱世，一生奋斗的目标是拨乱反正。他所思考的是当时面临的迫切问题，不大注意其他的问题，尤其是不实际的问题。他不谈怪和神 (7.21)，劝诫弟子不要去考虑鬼神和死后的事 (11.12)。换言之，他注重的是现实和人生。这种务实精神对中国人的性格和中国文化的特性有重大的影响。一个明显的表现是绝大多数中国人没有宗教信仰，更没有宗教狂热。

佛教从东汉初年，也就是公元初年，传入中国后，经过四、五百年的传播，影响逐步扩大，达到南北朝时期的兴盛，同时也遭到不断的批判。到唐朝，还有些佛教派别很有影响，宋以后就衰落下来。庙宇固然不少，但真正的信徒在人口中只是很小的一部分。

抵制和批判佛教最力的还是儒家。儒家继承孔子的思想，提倡忠孝和仁义：每个人对君主和父母都要承担义务，对国家的安危、民众的疾苦，要有责任感。这种现实的、入世的态度和佛教所宣扬的出世的、虚幻的思想完全相反。他们自然反对佛教。

道教是中国人创立的宗教，以清静无为为宗旨，同样与儒家的思想相抵触，因而也为儒家所反对。

从东汉到清末的两千年中，佛、道二教始终没有能压倒儒家思想，取得主导地位。由此可见儒家或孔子思想的无可比拟的力量。它强大，正因为它适应中国封建社会的要求，深深扎根于人们的思想之中。

世界上不少国家都发生过宗教战争，但中国没有发生过。

有人认为儒家也是一个宗教，可以和佛教、道教并列而为三教。

如果从孔子的思想在中国的影响看，其广泛的程度和时间的长久确和宗教有相似之处。但把孔子看作一个宗教的创始人是不恰当的，因为他们之间有根本的区别。

宗教的创建者总是自称或被认为是上帝的代言人，是与凡人不同的人。他传达上帝的意旨，教导人们去信仰上帝或神。他劝人为善，若是则死后可进天堂，否则便下地狱。他建立宗教组织，制定复杂的仪式和教规。

孔子不是这样。他说自己"吾少也贱，故多能鄙事；"（9.6）"我非生而知之者，好古敏以求之者也；"（7.20）"若圣与仁，则吾岂敢？"（7.34）可见他把自己看作一个普通人，不是上帝的代表。

孔子并不传达上帝的意旨。他讲的道理是从生活实际出发，解决实际问题的。他的目的是提高统治者和民众的道德水平，从而稳定社会秩序，改善国家的治理。他并不教导人们去信仰上帝，为今生或来生谋求幸福。历代中国人普遍地接受他的思想，主要因为人们认为他的思想是正确的，可实行的，有益于每个正直的人。

在孔子以后，每个时代都有儒家学者，他们努力传播他的思想，但并没有建立尊孔子为神或先知的宗教性组织。

今天，孔子的影响似乎不仅在中国，而且在许多别的亚洲国家，重新起作用。人们在谈论孔子思想推动了东亚一些国家和地区的迅速的发展,是治疗当前时代许多痼疾的良方。这是它的无穷的生命力和不可估量的力量的新的表现。它的力量正是来自它的务实精神。

一位宋儒曾说过:"天不生仲尼,万古长如夜。"这两句夸张的诗句表明很多人认为孔子明确了是非的界限,使得人们有所遵循,不再在黑暗中糊涂地摸索。我们今天对孔子思想应该采取研究分析、区别对待的态度,肯定其值得肯定的部分,舍弃其需要舍弃的部分;既不要认为他的观点是两千五百年前提出来的而都陈旧过时,也不要认为他所说的每句话在今天都仍然有效。

孔子提倡道德修养,提倡教育,提倡中庸与和谐,提倡务实,这些对中国人民素质的提高,对中国文化的发展,有很大的推动作用。他的治国主张,对礼的重视,对家庭的重视,既有助于中国社会长时间的和平与稳定,又延缓了中国社会的变革与发展。

A List of Names

Bigan: Uncle of the last king of the Shang dynasty.

Boqing: Son of the Duke of Zhou.

Boyi and Shuqi: Princes of a state in the Shang dynasty.

Cao Cao: Leader of the Kingdom of Wei during the period of the Three Kingdoms.

Chiyou: Legendary tribal leader.

Dong Zhuo: Man who had real control of the government towards the end of the Han dynasty.

Dong Zhongshu: Important Confucian scholar of the Han dynasty.

Duke Ai: Ruler of Lu.

Duke Huan: Ruler of Qi.

Duke Jing: Ruler of Qi.

Duke of Zhou: One of the founders of the Western Zhou dynasty.

Duke Wen: Ruler of Jin

Emperor Wudi: Emperor of the Western Han dynasty.

Fan Chi: Confucius' disciple.

Fuxi: Legendary tribal leader.

Gaoyao: Legendary leader Shun's assistant.

Gongxi Hua: Confucius' disciple.

Guan Zhong: Chief minister of Qi during Duke Huan's reign.

Guan Yu: Famous warrior during the period of the Three Kingdoms.

Huangdi: Yellow Emperor, a legendary tribal leader.

Ji : Legendary hero who taught people how to plant crops.

Ji Kang Zi: Nobleman of Lu.

Ji Lu: Another name of Zi Lu.

King Cheng: King of the Western Zhou dynasty.

King Ping: First king of the Eastern Zhou dynasty.

King Wen: Ruler of the state of Zhou before it conquered Shang.

King Wu: First king of the Western Zhou dynasty.

King You: Last king of the Western Zhou dynasty.

King Zhao: King of the state of Chu.

Kong Li: Confucius' son.

Kong Qiu: Original name of Confucius.

Kong Yu: Nobleman of Wei.

Kong Wen Zi: Posthumous title given to Kong Yu.

Li: Kong Li, Confucius' son.

Liuxia Hui: Virtuous man of Lu.

Mencius: Meng Zi, famous Confucian scholar of the Warring States Period. The book he wrote is entitled *The Mencius*.

Prince Jiu: Prince of Qi, killed by his brother Prince Xiaobai.

Prince Xiaobai: Prince of Qi; later ruler of the state known as Duke Huan.

Qi: Yu's son and successor, founder of the Xia dynasty.

Ran Qiu: Confucius' disciple.

Ran You: Another name of Ran Qiu.

Shang: another name of Zi Xia.

Shuliang He: Confucius' father.

Shuqi: See "Boyi and Shuqi".

Shi: Another name of Zi Zhang.

Shun: Ancient leader of the Chinese.

Shusun Wushu: Nobleman of Lu.

Sima Niu: Confucius' disciple.

Tang: Founder of the Shang dynasty.

Wudi: Emperor Wudi of the Han dynasty.

Xun Qing: Important Confucian scholar of the Warring States Period.

Yandi: Legendary tribal leader.

Yan Hui: Confucius' disciple.

Yan Lu: Confucius' disciple and Yan Hui's father.

Yan Pingzhong: Another name of Yan Ying.

Yan Yan: Confucius' disciple.

Yan Ying: Virtuous nobleman of Qi.

Yan Yuan: Another name of Yan Hui.

Yan Zhengzai: Confucius' mother.

Yao: Ancient leader of the Chinese.

Yi: Man chosen by Yu to be the latter's successor, but killed by Yu's son.

Youruo: Confucius' disciple.

You Zi: Another name of Youruo.

Yu: Ancient leader of the Chinese; said to have tamed serious floods.

Zai Wo: Another name of Zai Yu.

Zai Yu: Confucius' disciple.

Zeng Dian: Confucius' disciple and Zeng Shen's father.

Zeng Shen: Confucius' disciple.

Zeng Xi: Another name of Zeng Dian.

Zang Wenzhong: Nobleman of Lu.

Zhong Gong: Confucius' disciple.

Zhongni: Confucius' courtesy name.

Zhuge Liang: Chief minister of Shu during the period of the Three Kingdoms.

Zi Chan: Chief minister of the state of Zheng.

Zifu Jingbo: Nobleman of Lu.

Zi Gong: Confucius' disciple.

Zi Lu: Confucius' disciple.

Zi Wen: Chief minister of the state of Chu.

Zi Xi: Chief minister of the state of Chu.

Zi Xia: Confucius' disciple.

Zi You: Confucius' disciple.

Zi Zhang: Confucius' disciple.

人物表

比干：商纣王之叔。

伯禽：周公之子。

伯夷、叔齐：商朝孤竹国王子。

曹操：三国时期魏国的奠基者。

蚩尤：传说中的部落领袖。

董卓：东汉末年执掌朝政的军阀。

董仲舒：汉代的重要儒家学者。

鲁哀公：鲁国国君。

齐桓公：齐国国君。

齐景公：齐国国君。

周公：周朝的奠基人之一。

晋文公：晋国国君。

武帝：西汉皇帝。

樊迟：孔子的学生。

伏羲：传说中的部落领袖。

皋陶：舜的贤臣。

公西华：孔子的学生。

管仲：齐桓公的宰相。

关羽：三国时期蜀国大将。

黄帝：传说中的部落领袖。

稷：传说中教人稼穑的贤人。

季康子：鲁国贵族。

季路：子路的别字。

周成王：西周的君王。

周平王：东周的第一位君王。

周文王：周灭商之前的周国国君。

周武王：西周的第一位君王。

周幽王：西周的最后一位君王。

楚昭王：楚国国君。

孔鲤：孔子之子。

孔丘：孔子的原名。

孔圉：卫国的贵族。

孔文子：孔圉的谥号。

鲤：即孔鲤，孔子之子。

柳下惠：鲁国的贤人。

孟子：孟轲，战国时著名的儒家学者，他的著作名为
《孟子》。

公子纠: 齐国公子, 被他的哥哥公子小白所杀。

公子小白: 齐国公子, 后来成为齐国国君, 即齐桓公。

启: 大禹之子, 后继承父位, 成为夏朝的第一位君王。

冉求: 孔子的学生。

冉有: 冉求之字。

商: 子夏之名。

叔梁纥: 孔子之父。

叔齐: 见"伯夷、叔齐"。

师: 子张之名。

舜: 古时的部落领袖。

叔孙武叔: 鲁国贵族。

司马牛: 孔子的学生。

汤: 商代开国君王。

汉武帝: 汉代皇帝。

荀卿: 战国时期著名的儒家学者。

炎帝: 传说中的部落领袖。

颜回: 孔子的学生。

颜路: 孔子的学生, 颜回之父。

晏平仲: 晏婴之字。

言偃: 孔子的学生。

晏婴: 齐国的贤相。

颜渊: 颜回之字。

颜徵在: 孔子之母。

尧: 古时的部落领袖。

益：禹所挑选的继承人，后被禹子启所杀。

有若：孔子的学生。

有子：有若的尊称。

禹：古时的部落领袖，传说曾治服洪水。

宰我：宰予的别称。

宰予：孔子的学生。

曾点：孔子的学生，曾参之父。

曾参：孔子的学生。

曾皙：曾点之字。

臧文仲：鲁国贵族。

仲弓：孔子的学生。

仲尼：孔子之字。

诸葛亮：三国时期蜀国的贤相。

子产：郑国的贤相。

子服景伯：鲁国贵族。

子贡：孔子的学生。

子路：孔子的学生。

子文：楚国的令尹。

子西：楚国的令尹。

子夏：孔子的学生。

子游：即言偃，孔子的学生。

子张：孔子的学生。

图书在版编目 (CIP) 数据

孔子新评：英、汉对照/丁往道著译．—北京：中国文学出版社，1997.3
ISBN 7-5071-0383-8

Ⅰ.孔… Ⅱ.丁… Ⅲ.孔丘-思想评论-对照物—英、汉 Ⅳ.B.222.2

中国版本图书馆 CIP 数据核字 (96) 第 24929 号

孔子新评

著译者　丁往道
中文责编　孙国勇
英文责编　章思英
熊猫丛书
*
中国文学出版社
（中国北京百万庄路 24 号）
中国国际图书贸易总公司发行
（中国北京车公庄西路 35 号）
北京邮政信箱第 339 号　邮政编码 100044
1997 年第 1 版（英、汉对照）
ISBN 7-5071-0383-8
02800
10-EC-3144P